PENGUIN

EGGS FOR DINNER

Born in 1971 in Haifa Israel, Guy Wachs grew up immersed in the family's hospitality business and went on to train in hospitality administration and management in Germany at the prestigious Hotelfachschule Villingen-Schwenningen. Having developed a passion for fine wine and dining and armed with his new professional skills, Guy moved to New York City where he gained more experience in well-known establishments like the iconic Cafe Luxembourg and then Cafe Centro, winning awards along the way for his innovation.

Guy moved to Asia in 2004 and began working in Bangkok for the Singapore based Raffles Hotel Group. A subsequent move to Singapore led to the opening of his own restaurant, Wild Honey in 2009. Since then, Guy's business has expanded into three popular outlets. Guy now spends his time managing his restaurants and mentoring budding entrepreneurs and guest speaking at the Singapore Management University and the Culinary Institute of Singapore. On weekends, Guy can be found bike riding around the coast of Singapore and enjoying experimenting with new culinary creations to introduce to his loyal customers.

Today, some thirteen years later in a post-Covid world, Guy has rewritten the rule book of how to operate and keep sane in a business so dependent on adapting and remaining agile. Singapore continues to be home, but Guy is infused with optimism and hopes that perhaps Wild Honey may cross Singapore's borders and open overseas.

Eggs for Dinner
A Restaurateur Who Sees
The World Differently

Guy Wachs

PENGUIN BOOKS

An imprint of Penguin Random House

PENGUIN BOOKS

USA | Canada | UK | Ireland | Australia
New Zealand | India | South Africa | China | Southeast Asia

Penguin Books is part of the Penguin Random House group of companies
whose addresses can be found at global.penguinrandomhouse.com

Published by Penguin Random House SEA Pvt. Ltd
9, Changi South Street 3, Level 08-01,
Singapore 486361

First published in Penguin Books by Penguin Random House SEA 2023

Copyright © Guy Wachs 2023
The author acknowledges Sumati Sachdev is the writer of this work.

ISBN 9789815058925

Typeset in Adobe Caslon Pro by MAP Systems, Bangalore, India

www.penguin.sg

For my Wild Honey team

Contents

Chapter 1

All Stop

Wild Honey opened its doors on Orchard Road, the heart of the shopping and dining district of Singapore, in 2009. Ten years later, as Singapore and the rest of the world faced the threat of Covid-19, it was forced to close its doors. A desperate fear reverberated through the service industry, reflected in the deafening silence on Orchard Road. Wild Honey at Mandarin Gallery overlooked this thoroughfare. Directly opposite was what used to be the iconic Robinsons shopping centre, established in 1858. Takashimaya was to its left and the Mandarin Orchard Hotel just above. The hum of traffic, the gridlock of cars and the throngs that habitually inhabited the busiest shopping street in Singapore had disappeared overnight.

When the Singapore government acted, the changes were abrupt. A circuit breaker, announced on 3 April 2020 by Singapore's Prime Minister Lee Hsien Loong, was to take effect on 7 April for a month. Three days. That is all the notice we had. It had different names in different countries, but essentially, this was the start of lockdowns worldwide. People were to work from home, schools shifted to home-based learning, and only places providing essential services could continue to operate. Social gatherings in private and public spaces were now prohibited, and travel became problematic. Most significant for us was that dining-in at eateries was prohibited. However, since we were considered an essential service, we could stay open for takeaway and deliveries. I simultaneously went into overdrive and intense self-reflection. Within twenty-four hours, Wild Honey went online 24/7. We opened up island-wide delivery and, to deal with the intense anxiety I was feeling, I started to write.

Then, on 21st April, the circuit breaker was extended till 1st June, and the restrictions tightened even further. The number of essential businesses allowed to operate was narrowed and there were even entry restrictions imposed at wet markets and supermarkets. Standalone outlets—selling only beverages, packaged snacks, confectioneries, or desserts—had to close their retail shops. Online sales were allowed but only if the food items were sold from a licensed central kitchen, manufacturing facility, or warehouse. Sites that produced cakes, ice cream, and chocolate were banned from operating, and home-based businesses were not allowed to operate. It was the death of retail.

The deserted streets gave me flashbacks of the 1991 Gulf War when I was living in Israel. We had scuds missiles falling on us—not knowing if they were chemical warheads—and we were told that if we did not have our gasmasks on, we were toast. So, I learned the mask lesson when I was young. I remembered 9/11 when I was living and working in New York, and after the towers fell, we all became paranoid. We had these wacky people calling up the restaurant with fake bomb threats and we would have to evacuate in the middle of meals. This global pandemic brought similar feelings of anxiety, and I felt lonely and very scared. Yet, strangely, I felt reassured at the same time, as facing challenges and fighting battles put me in my element.

If the past three years have taught us anything, it is to always expect the unexpected in life. I never anticipated becoming a restaurant owner, could not have foreseen in my wildest dreams that the retail industry would ever totally shut down worldwide, and never thought I would write this book. I sat in my restaurant the day after the announcement of an island-wide circuit breaker; the quietness was eerie; the atmosphere post-apocalyptic. Strangely, almost as soon as the country went into a lockdown, I noticed a couple would walk down Orchard Road every day, dressed identically in Adidas tracksuits with cleanly shaven heads. It gave me a feeling of aliens having landed. I shuddered and wondered if we would ever open our doors again. I believed that my restaurant would more likely swim, meaning survive, than sink. With loyal staff dependent on Wild Honey, and ten years of our own emotional and physical investment, I knew that sinking was not an option.

Ask any entrepreneur what they thrive on, and the answer is likely to include 'facing difficulty'. It is where the best ideas come from; innovation and creativity thrive when one is faced with worst case scenarios. As the Jews say, *never miss the opportunity of a good disaster.* My instincts told me that no matter what, we were going to get through this and would emerge from the pandemic even stronger than before.

This is the story of Wild Honey, Singapore. A lifestyle brand and the first all-day-breakfast restaurant in Singapore, created by my wife Stephanie and I. It is the story of our journey, taking an idea, a passion, and turning it into a successful business. This is also the story of a humble Jewish dishwasher who achieved his dream of being a successful restaurateur on the tiny powerhouse, the Southeast Asian Island of Singapore.

Young people have often asked me three basic questions about opening a restaurant.

1. How do I finance it?
2. Who should I work with?
3. What does it take to become successful?

Hopefully, the experiences related in this book will help those considering a profession in the Food and Beverage Industry and will help answer those questions.

* * *

Covid-19 has taught us that experts do matter. I had the privilege of beginning my journey towards becoming an expert when I did my three-year-long Hotelfachmann Apprenticeship in Baden-Baden, Germany, from 1991 to 1993. This apprenticeship was based on the classic model, which has been widespread throughout Europe for centuries. This is a dual education system where professional job training is accompanied by studies and it is almost impossible to get a job without it. The basis of it is to train a new generation of practitioners and is funded by the state and the employers. So, I got a free education. How cool is that? In many places now this has been replaced by academic theory. I believe that in my profession, there is no substitute for doing time. You do not become an expert overnight, and it involves a time consuming and laborious process. In Roger Kneebone's book *Expert*, he describes the process of becoming an expert in three steps: Apprentice—Journeyman—Expert. I believe that I have achieved this status of an expert.

To be of service is a mindset where you have to breathe, crawl, walk, climb, sleep, and then dream service, and there is no better way to do this than through experience. During the apprenticeship phase, I looked inwards and tried to practice the skills needed in the art of hospitality. After my apprenticeship, my next phase was as a journeyman. I started working in 1994 and this is when I became more aware of the people around me and began to develop my own voice and style. Becoming an Expert has been all about learning to troubleshoot and make critical but often unorthodox decisions quickly. As an expert in my field, I have assembled a team I can trust, which has created the space for me to be creative and innovative. This has meant that I have been able to become a restaurateur as opposed to just being able to emulate restaurateurs.

Over the years, demands and trends have changed, but one thing remains true: context is everything. In Asia, once a dinner is completed, meals are expected to be cleared immediately, whereas in the West, it would be a faux pas. French service uses large elaborate trays that are presented with panache, before serving from the left. English service entails rolling trolleys to guests and cutting the roast beef as part of the experience. Russian service, similar to Asia, works by placing portions for sharing in the middle of the table from where guests serve themselves, and American service is the opposite: food is plated in the kitchen and served individually. So, which one is correct? In my opinion, the one that works. In other words, what remains true is adapting, being creative, and anticipating change. This is the key to survival.

The difference between a good restaurant and a great restaurant depends on thousands of details. 'Embrace failure,' says Thomas Keller, the chef known for the acclaimed French Laundry, Per Se, and Bouchon Bakery. Thomas Keller has won the James Beard award, the Oscar of the culinary world. What people do not know is that his first restaurant in New York was a flop. As a talented restaurant manager, you must be prepared to fall and get up. You need to master purchasing, negotiating, logistics, cooking, mixology, human resource training, marketing, and public relations. Most importantly, you have to be an ace in guest service. You are like a head nurse taking care of people while they eat and play, demand your attention, and expect devotion and care. They need to feel safe and comfortable. It is no surprise that the first flight attendants on Qantas were called Flying Nurses. Whenever you visit somewhere, whether it is a hotel, a restaurant, or a home, you want to feel safe and taken care of, and I do not think there is anything special in providing that; it should be natural.

Restaurants are also about theatre and drama. My first fine dining experience was in New York at the Union Pacific Restaurant. To enter the dining room, guests walked through a waterfall. The service staff were polished and polite and as they began to serve us each dish paired with the appropriate wine, we could see the culinary staff's shadows through the frosted windows. The effect was of dancers in a smoothly flowing movement, synchronized perfectly. It was a sensory overload for the taste buds, but also visually and emotionally delightful, creating an enchanting experience. The opposite end of this was my experience in Tokyo where cooking is done at live stations, and every time guests entered and left, the chefs would shout in unison to greet and thank them.

Diners want to be noticed and want to remember their experience. If people just wanted food, they would go to the supermarket. Good restaurateurs understand this and create magical spaces. This is what is behind the success of Wild Honey; we have created a strong brand identity driven by our distinct design elements that make us stand out from other restaurants. *Wild Honey—No place Like Home* is not just a restaurant but a destination where people feel welcome and relaxed in an eclectic, classic, and relaxed environment. Today, with three distinct outlets, I can proudly say we have fulfilled our aims. But, in business, the target is always moving.

Restaurants also have to innovate to survive. Wild Honey managed to stay ahead of the curve during the ongoing pandemic. Imagine, the last time hotels and restaurants shut down like this was during World War II, so there was much to learn from the shutdown. Life slowed down, there was less pollution, and the connection between the environment and the food became more important to people. The future of food and beverage might not be restaurants as we know them today as the market will evolve and restaurateurs have to anticipate new platforms. Having said that, good fortune beats any plan, and I have had the good fortune of having Stephanie to watch my back and the honour of being mentored by many talented people. I also have being a restaurateur in my blood. My father Gabriel was a restaurateur before me. He taught me how to connect with people, how to innovate, and he gave me the drive to succeed.

Chapter 2

Haifa to California—*Oy Vay!*

Haifa! The Northern Israeli port city that embraced all religions—Muslims, Christians, and Jews—and where I had the honour of being born. In 1971, there were not many places to go to in this sleepy city. It did not have the sex appeal of Tel Aviv or spiritualism of Jerusalem; but as a place to grow up, it was sublime. This is where I lived with my parents—Gabriel and Lisa. My early memories were blissfully happy. My father remembers me as a beautiful angel with a very good nature, and I remember Haifa as a little paradise.

As a toddler, my parents would often take me to a small cabana they owned on Carmel beach, a picturesque strip of shoreline facing the Mediterranean Sea. To me, as a little boy, it was just impossibly vast, offering all the possibilities a child could desire. I was a natural swimmer, and my parents were friends with the lifeguards; so, they would let me go out on the paddle boats, which no other children were allowed to do. I used to feel very special. The Mediterranean Sea had its own distinctive quality, a personality forged over millennia in this historic and spiritual region. We would drive down to the cabana from our house on Carmel Mountain, which had a panoramic view of the Beach, the bay, and the port. On a clear day, you could see all the way to the north of Israel. For a young boy, it felt like this was the whole world.

In Haifa, we had a supportive community around us and the constant smell of the ocean. In those years, life was dominated by my parents, our Volvo station wagon, and Noor, our German Shepherd. Noor loved to swim in the Mediterranean, and, after a nice day at the beach, we would drive back home with Noor running behind the car. My recollections, though sometimes vague, always have a quality of calm and sweetness to them. When we were not at the beach, I would sit on the patio of our apartment on the mountainside and wait for the garbage truck. I was fascinated by that truck, and every time I saw it, I would run out and make them stop. I would, then, climb on top to play with the steering wheel. It was my truck-mania phase; the first of my many manias in my life that progressed into different kinds of obsessions. I can be very extreme about my likes and dislikes and find it very hard to settle on any middle ground. In later years, this character trait would serve me well in my career.

* * *

Those early years in Haifa were where my exposure to the restaurant world began. I spent a lot of my time in Café Carmel, a Viennese style cafe situated in Haifa, and one of the most elegant places on Mt. Carmel. The café had been in our family since it opened in the 1930s, entertaining British army officers, writers, artists, and local Europeans. It belonged to my great uncle and aunt—Alfred and Valliy Tychner. Gabriel had dreams of running it from a young age. Fate intervened to make it happen. After vocational school in Israel, he had gone to Germany to study baking and culinary and had then attended a hotel school in Tegernsee. In 1968, his uncle and aunt tragically died in a plane crash on a visit to Europe, and as my father's background was in hospitality, it was natural that he would inherit the café.

So, when he took over the café, my father had the right training to run a successful restaurant. He bought new equipment and furniture and revamped the menu. Cakes were a mainstay as would be expected in a café, and the specialty was apple cake. Not the usual apple pie but instead apple cake that infused the aroma of cinnamon and cloves into the classic cedar oak furniture that inhabited the cafe. This was just the start of his ambitious and creative streak. He introduced crêpes suzette to the Haifa crowd along with French toast and his unusual hardboiled egg and cheese toasted sandwiches smothered with a creamy mushroom sauce. Burnt coffee wafted down the street drawing crowds, and the food was so tasty that people began fighting over tables at the weekend, and very quickly, it became, as my father calls it, the spotlight of the town. And why would it not? White marble tabletops with a gothic ceiling welcomed the clientele along with a large flower arrangement at the entrance, like a five-star hotel! When you sat at your table, your food would arrive down a dummy waiter pulled by ropes. It was quaint and majestic, and the pastries were to die for. It became so famous that anyone who was anyone would end up at Café Carmel.

As a young boy, naturally, I would visit my father at the café where I would be treated to Black Forest cakes and Kinley orange soda. It was there that I first fell in love with the smell of coffee, even though I would not taste it for a few more years. As a boy, it was the vibrant warm environment created by Gabriel's charm and good humour that had the strongest impact on me. Many of the guests were regulars and enjoyed conversing with him on various topics. Some wanted to discuss politics, others wanted to talk about sports. Gabriel read widely and taught me that a person should be able to converse with knowledge about any topic. He spoke so many languages—Hebrew, English, German, French, and even some Italian—that no one was left out of the banter.

Sometimes, when he was in the mood, he would play live music with his band. He was proficient on the guitar and drums, was always full of energy and loved being the boss who was able to do whatever he wanted at the café. He would cook, wash the dishes, make the coffee and serve, and clear at a moment's notice. Café Carmel was a joyful place where Gabriel made the patrons feel at ease, and I watched with wonder as my father got paid to make people feel good. I did not know it then but I was getting my first lesson in how to run an owner-operated enterprise.

Owning his own cafe allowed Gabriel to flex his creative muscles. He started to hold all kinds of events there, including a fashion show with beautiful young models, which was a real hit. The mayor of the city, Moshe Flieman, was a committed gourmet, and every Friday he would appear at the café with his friends where they would take over the kitchen and cook for themselves. The newspapers loved this unusual drama of a politician and prominent members of society pitching up at this small café, adorning aprons and cooking up a storm. The papers featured them on a long table feasting on their three-hour-long lunches. It was food, politics, friendship, and pleasure all rolled into one. This was my introduction to the enticing world of hospitality.

Another lesson I learned young was watching my father's staff become his friends. I remember he had a dishwasher called Abdallah who looked like Charlie Chaplin and had a limp. We were invited into his home for his son Gilad's wedding, and I was given a green chilli that scorched my mouth. Pita bread and Coca-Cola were offered, in good humour, to put out the fire and that memory remains as vivid as the dignity of the people my father introduced me to. This camaraderie stayed with me and became the cornerstone of how I relate to, judge, and choose my colleagues and friends.

Unfortunately, in many ways, Haifa was too small and provincial for my father, Gabriel. He had this itch to travel and explore. He was also not wholly comfortable under the watchful eye of his mother—my grandmother—Edith, or as we say in Hebrew, Sabta, as he needed total creative freedom to thrive. Israel was particularly affected after the Yom Kippur War of 1973, and my parents felt disillusioned and trapped in Israel running the cafe. This was the beginning of about eight years of scuttling back and forth between the US and Israel.

In 1974, we moved to Hawaii where my father got a job managing a restaurant and my most vivid memory is the smell of coconut oil and vertigo as I peered over the edge of the balcony where my father had roughly tossed away my pacifier. Although this was short lived, for just a year, whenever the nutty smell of coconut oil is around, a sense of foreboding accompanies it. My parents returned to Israel for my brother Daniel's birth in 1976, and my father began a series of jobs managing restaurants in hotels and actually remembers that period fondly. He often talks of the events he ran, creating new concepts and implementing these ideas. Still, there was obviously some bug in him; I call it the 'must open my own restaurant bug' because he kept returning to the US in search of that dream.

Looking back, it was the calm before the storm. Once we embarked on the incessant moving, and then the birth of my younger brother Daniel, my life changed dramatically as we were totally alone.

* * *

As new immigrants to the US, life was lonely and challenging. We lived in Tiburon in Marin County, which, being near the bay, should have given me some sense of familiarity and comfort. It did not because the place had no soul at all. Living in Tiburon was like being in a prison for me. There was no life in the streets, the weather was foggy and cold, and the people kept their distance. The area we lived in was full of large mansions and people stayed behind closed doors, so it felt isolated. Our house was small, basic, and being on the bay, I would ride my BMX along the bike path by the shore and look for crabs under the rocks. I remember many long hours playing with my Lego and car collection. Most of all, I remember being alone. For my father, the commute to work was long. He worked night and day, and we never saw him.

I felt uprooted. The 1970s in San Francisco was rocking. It was the rainbow capital of the world with gay marches, big Harley Davidsons zooming through the city, and open air jacuzzis. In hindsight, a great happening place, but for a sheltered young boy from Haifa, it was too much for me to take in all at once. School was often unpleasant. I struggled with my academics and was more interested in making friends, but that was also difficult as I was an outcast with a name like 'Gal'. Even that which should have been positive never quite worked out right. My father, who was always good with his hands, bought an old boat and renovated it. One day, we went out on the boat, named G & D (my brother Daniel and my initials) into the San Francisco Bay and we all ended up with carbon monoxide poisoning, only just managing to make it back to the Marina in Tiburon. I have had an aversion to sailing ever since. I did enjoy learning judo, but then that got too physical for my taste. Then I played soccer as a goalkeeper and I was not bad, but never quite felt part of the team. I was an outsider everywhere now. The more I tried to make friends, the worse it got.

Luckily, I had a neighbour named Guy Yost, who was a few years older than me and spent his time teaching me to build models, listen to rock music, and ride a BMX cycle. This was a welcome and rare friendship in those years. I was so unhappy it seemed to taint everything. Eventually, I managed to gain a few more friends and I remember one of them, David, lived right next to the San Quentin Prison. Sometimes, when we played together, the prison bus would stop directly in front of his house. An unforgettable image for me was the prisoners' shadows that seemed to stare at me, and I at them, terrified. It was a meaningless childhood fear but seemed to reflect the general unease and unhappiness I felt. The atmosphere at home was toxic. My parents were constantly fighting about money and it was always a loud and violent conflict, a memory that has stayed with me. Those years in San Francisco were dark years for me.

Meanwhile, despite all the challenges of dislocating the family, Gabriel's dream remained to open his own restaurant. He hoped to open a chain of Middle Eastern restaurants in America and had the innovative concept of a fast-food style vegetarian menu located in the Central Business District area of San Francisco. His dream materialized in the form of 'Pita Pocket Place'. The restaurant focused on Israeli food and particularly on falafels. What was interesting was that my father was as concerned with the experience of eating as he was with the quality of the food. He realized that the falafel had a particular problem of being held and eaten without creating a mess, so he designed a special support plate and a stand so customers could balance the pita and falafel on the stand like a sandwich. That attention to detail was astonishing in those days. Today, designing and sourcing the right containers to pack food in and eat from is a multimillion dollar business in itself and this was just another example of how he was such a visionary.

However, these were early days for American health food consciousness in California, which was still dominated by fast food and diners. This would change later and California would be at the forefront of the farm-to-table concept with trailblazers like chef and author Alice Waters—the founder of Chez Panisse Restaurant in Berkeley, California—paving the way. Back in

1975, there were very few fresh markets and sustainable eating was not recognized or understood, nor the connection between food and health. It is such a shame that my father's restaurant concept did not take off because, for poor Americans, fast food was the only affordable option, and my father's new venture was fast, cheap, sustainable, and healthy. It was too unfamiliar to Americans, and they were just not willing to try.

After five years, Pita Pocket Place went bankrupt. *Oy gevalt!* Running a cafe in Haifa had not prepared my father for the business environment in San Francisco. Then, there was the food. People did not understand it because it was too exotic and foreign for them. Before leaving for the USA, I had seen my father working on the concept, the menu, and the costing. There seemed to be no reason that items like pita bread and hummus and falafel balls, offered in restaurants all over the world today, would not be popular. Unfortunately, the city was wrong for this venture. There was a large Asian population in San Francisco, but who was going to eat vegetarian food? The point was that he had not thought this through. Then, when he was finally noticed by the large Safeway supermarket chain, he was unprepared as without a production kitchen, he could not handle the orders. It was unfortunate and, in retrospect, he was thirty years ahead of his time. Watching my family go through financial ruin would shape me for the rest of my life. They had gambled everything on this business and left no safety net, but it was the shame that I could sense in my father that really affected me. For many years, I was terrified of risk. In fact, I was terrified of the whole restaurant business, and, for a long time, I was very certain I never wanted to own my own business. I felt very sorry for my father, watching his American dream fail, and it was clear America was not working for any of us. I was very homesick and just wanted to go back to Haifa.

After Pita Pocket Place closed, we returned to Israel to start again from nothing.

Chapter 3

Return to Israel

The American experiment was over. For my father, it was devastating, but for me, the dream had always been to return home; so, I was thrilled. Little did I know that the turmoil that began with that first move to America would follow me back home to Israel.

My parents remained in the US to finish up packing to relocate back to Israel, but I was eager to return. Being only eleven years old, they requested my Hebrew teacher from Brandeis Hillel School to chaperone me as she was also travelling back for her home leave. We boarded a Trans World Airlines flight to return to Israel. I was excited about travelling with my teacher and was looking forward to the trip back home. I remembered my Sabta Edith's home; the family home where my father and his brother Rafi had grown up. The thought of returning there filled me with joy because it was the nourishment I craved after the loneliness I had experienced in America. Her relationship with my father might have been fraught, but towards me, she was always warm and comforting.

Sabta Edith's house held many good memories for me. Before the US 'adventure', I had spent many hours in the basement, which was also where Uncle Rafi's dental practice was situated. Uncle Rafi was my father's brother and his dental practice gave the basement that biting sharp reek of chemical and plastic that seems to hang in the air of all medical practitioners' waiting rooms. I remember Uncle Rafi would speak very softly to his patients using that Wach's charm. He had giant beds that would keep the patients perfectly still while he worked on their teeth, and he would go from one bed to the next, sometimes doing up to seven patients at the same time! He was a true expert in his field and I remember feeling proud to be his nephew.

Magazines and books decorated the bookshelves and there was an eye-catching large aquarium with colourful exotic fish and the centrepiece, a glass table with games and toys for children to play with. My favourite was a maze board with a metal ball. The quintessential waiting room children's toy! I could sit for hours manoeuvring the ball through each twist and turn, fascinated by the simple gliding mechanism. I enjoyed it because it had a clear starting point, a definable goal that I understood, and it was safe and manageable. Then, to top it all off as the ideal play area for children, there was a secret door that led upstairs to the house above that Rafi would slip out from to join his beautiful wife Judy in the kitchen on the floor above.

My favourite part of the house was the kitchen as it always had my Sabta in it and the smells promised the comfort of her cooking. There, I would eat dumplings with apricot and cinnamon, a dish from the Czech Republic, where my Sabta was originally from. The living room had an imposing white grand piano and oversized oil paintings with dramatic representations from biblical times. Directly above the living room was my Sabta's bedroom, where, in the midst of all this history and culture, sat her spinning bicycle. Gabriel's room was next door and up above, right at the top of the house was the attic where she did all of the household's laundry. As a young boy, I would wait for a new box of detergent to be opened and avidly collect the free gift toy soldiers inside to play with. The house smelled like old wood. The garden needed constant attention and I would help Sabta water the plants with a yellow watering can, which I would struggle to carry but refused help when offered. The house may have been cozy and comforting, but for a child, it was exciting, mysterious, and pulsating with the potential of adventure. I was elated to be returning to the security and wonder of Sabta's house.

* * *

In 1982, my teacher and I arrived at Haifa airport from the US. Waiting for the luggage felt like an eternity. I could not wait to get back to the views of the Mediterranean Sea, the comfort of Sabta Edith's home, and the familiar smells from the kitchen. We took a short taxi journey, and I recall chattering away to my teacher, unable to contain my excitement. Located on a steep hill, I always enjoyed that feeling of approaching the house from a height and watching it loom into view. As we turned the corner onto Mt Carmel, I sat up eagerly in the taxi, anticipating that sight. I could not see it. The taxi pulled up at 6A Hatzvi Street but there was nothing there. Just an empty plot of land.

Disoriented from the flight, I thought I had the wrong address and I scrambled around, frantically looking, while the taxi driver and my teacher waited patiently. I was young and without my family, so they gave me some time to gather myself. They also had no idea what was happening. It slowly became clear I was at the right address, but the house was no longer there. I was in shock and felt like I was sinking. For years, I had just wanted to come home. My only memory of that traumatic moment was the overwhelming desire to throw up. It was not that she had moved or that it was empty, but it had literally disappeared. In its place sat a barren flattened plot of land. Bewildered and frightened, in a confusing blur of memories,

I vaguely remember my Uncle Rafi being called to come and pick me up, and I was taken, strangely, just a few plots down the street, to a flat.

It transpired that Uncle Rafi had demolished the house with the intention of building a new home, and this flat was temporary accommodation for all of us. I was never told this but picked this up slowly from listening to snatches of conversations around the flat. Later, I understood that with my Sabta often being away in Switzerland and our family having moved to America, I suppose Uncle Rafi felt that this house was his to do with as he wished since his business was located within it. Honestly, the complexities of the division of family property were something I, as an eleven-year-old, could not comprehend. I would never end up understanding it even as an adult because, to this day, no one has ever spoken to me about what happened. There has always been silence from Uncle Rafi and Aunt Judy, my Sabta has now passed away, and Rafi and Gabriel still hardly speak to each other forty years later. It took this one incident to break a relationship that had been close and affectionate until that point. As an adult, looking back, I now understand the heart wrenching issues of inheritance and how it can break families. Once that summer of 1982 ended, the issue was bottled up like so many of the most difficult family problems; put in the metaphorical basement, and the door shut forever.

So, I had returned to Israel having been told by my parents to go straight to Sabta's house, and I was not quite sure at this point what I was supposed to do. You have an inkling as a child, an instinct, that something terrible is happening but, of course, you have no control. I wondered at the time if my parents knew that the house was gone. Did my Sabta know? Where would we live? My parents knew I had arrived safely, just not the fact that I was not in the family home. For two months I stayed at Uncle Rafi's flat, living in a sort of fearful, suspended reality. I did not have the comfort of the familiar house, I was numbed by the feeling that I needed to tell my parents the house was gone because I knew this situation would be the final blow to what was already going to be a very difficult homecoming for them, having had to close the failed business. I was too paralysed with fear and uncertainty to say anything to anyone about what had happened.

At the end of the summer, my parents were due to return. On the day they were expected back, I waited at the site of my Sabta's land for them to arrive. It was left for me to face them alone as they pulled up to the house and were confronted with the same sight that I had been greeted with two months earlier. Shock. In a classic "kill the messenger" moment, they decided the whole thing was my fault. Somehow, in their eyes, I had caused this whole catastrophe as I had not informed them that the house was gone and all that remained was an empty plot. As family drama goes, this one was nuclear. Not young enough to be oblivious and not quite old enough to be able to detach myself, I watched this unfold against the backdrop of the war in Lebanon and the echo of bombs punctuating our days and nights. My parents had run from the Yom Kippur War, only to return to two wars—one at "home" and another unfolding in the country.

This was not the homecoming I had foreseen, and I felt like I would never reclaim the happiness I had felt in those early years. Despite Uncle Rafi having rented a place to accommodate all of us, my parents categorically refused to go to that apartment. My parents' anger and pride resulted in us being effectively homeless for some time after this. Like vagabonds, we shifted from one rented accommodation to another, my father struggling to find work and me feeling pushed and pulled from the constant movement of our family from one place to another as he changed jobs. I never got a chance to drop anchor again in Israel, and in fact, it was only years later, returning there in my adulthood, that it began to feel like home again.

Tumult just kept following me, and even two years later, when I turned thirteen, my bar mitzvah was a terrible experience. This is such a significant event in a Jewish boy's life, but since it was still so tense between the families, I was a bundle of nerves and ended up losing my voice. Imagine my uncle's family and our family together with neither side speaking to each other. All eyes were on me while both sides avoided the other, silent and cold. My family and relatives were a microcosm of the surroundings, uncertainty, animosity, and war. This was Israel in 1984. In others around me I could see safety within the family. I saw how the community would retreat into spirituality for strength and support, especially when surrounded by the constant chaos of war, but it just did not seem available for me. I retreated further into my shell, rode my BMX bike, played basketball, and discovered Duran Duran.

My father still could not settle down, and after a few more jobs here and there, it was déjà vu for me as my family once again moved to California in 1987. I could not believe it was happening again. It felt like I was in a recurring nightmare. I was in my first year of high school, and it was particularly disruptive. My parents enrolled me in Redwood High School in Marin County, which was a public school rife with the issues that public schools face. I not only did not fit into any group, being an immigrant, but I was an introvert, lacked confidence (made worse by stress acne), and refused to take drugs. My home life paralleled the isolation I felt at school as my father was busy trying to repair our house to flip it for money. So we only had beds to sleep on and were like squatters in our own home. Without Duran Duran and David Bowie, I am unsure how I would have survived. Thankfully, this only lasted a year, the entire endeavour was a train wreck, and, before long, we were back in Israel.

* * *

The loss of Pita Pocket Place, the constant job uncertainty, and the back and forth between America and Israel were huge blows to my father's self-confidence. It was not until quite a few years later, when he landed a job at a respectable hotel in a Red Sea resort city, did some stability re-emerge for him, and consequently us. As the hotel manager of the Moriah Plaza hotel in Eilat, he oversaw the catering of important state events like the signing of a peace treaty between Jordan and Israel, with President Clinton presiding and attended by the King of Jordan and the late Prime Minister of Israel, Yitzak Rabin. What made him really settle down was that he could finally use his creativity again. The results were very apparent, and while there, he created one of the best food programmes in the city and won several awards. In a gratifying twist, I later helped my father get a job in New York City at the Sheraton, his last job before he retired. When I look back at his career; being ahead of the curve, innovative, creative thinker, and problem solver; this all made him untraditional. He was a risktaker and despite my personal difficulties with all the uprooting from one place to another, I look back on his approach as a glorious thing because, to be honest, I got all these traits from him.

Back in Israel in 1986 for the second time, I was privileged to attend A.I.S., the American International School, joining in Grade 10. While my father finally settled down working as an executive, I discovered the pleasure of reading for the first time, thanks to my English teacher, Joseph Bearman, who exposed me to American classics like *Catcher in the Rye*, and *Lord of the Flies*, and the works of Victor Hugo. I was introduced to and developed an interest in social justice, and I loved the stories about people overcoming the odds and finding happiness. These books opened up my imagination and took me to faraway places. Still, even with this stability and my growing interest in reading, my academic life did not improve. This in part, I learned later, was because I was dyslexic. So, 9 would become 6 and I would write an *F* but get a *T*. It was a pattern that had followed me through schools, and the constant relocations and always being the new kid in the class just added to the difficulties. Through some miracle and a tutor here and there, I did manage to graduate by the skin of my teeth, thanks to my math tutor, professor Joe Lyss. That seemed like the end of my academic life as it was quite apparent that school was just not my scene.

I finally left my parents' home when I was seventeen. The fighting and conflict had made me become self-destructive. I was angry and hurt. My parents were fully funding and supporting my musically gifted brother, but since my grades in school were very bad, they took little interest in my prospects. Instead of studies, socializing and surfing on Herzliya beach were my preferences. I became best friends with Rene Esfandi, and we bonded over backgammon matches. Rene was a wily gambling shark, three years older than me. We drove his father's Mercedes 190E and hit the clubs hard. It was the late 80s— Scirocco, Penguin, Timeout, and the Colosseum were the places to be seen at. When I finally graduated high school in 1989, I began working as a bartender in a pride bar called Queenie and had my first serious relationship with NG, which, of course, left me with a broken heart, as most first loves and break ups do. During this time, I also became friends with Boaz Dolgin, who was 20 years older and educated in London and Paris. Boaz was born with a golden spoon in his mouth. His father was the owner of the Ben Yehuda Cinema and a big-time contractor responsible for projects such as the Lechi Museum in Jaffa. Fortuitously, Boaz was a great foodie and would entertain Rene and me with scrumptious cuisine. The three of us became such good friends that years later, when I turned thirty, they both turned up in New York for my birthday and took me to Vegas for a week of fun. Since then, it has become a tradition for us to celebrate our birthdays together, and even when I moved to Asia, they flew out and we had great fun celebrating my fortieth in Singapore and Bangkok.

In 1989, straight after school, like all young men in Israel, I joined the Israel Defense Force for my civil service. Regretfully, my struggles followed me into the army, and after three months, I was discharged. I had been experimenting with drugs in grade twelve and was not prepared mentally and physically to become a soldier. I was not living with my parents, and after training, I had no safety net to fall back on. I got a panic attack and tried to run away, and finally they let me go. Disgraced for not completing my three years of service, my self-esteem lay bare on the floor. As an Israeli, this was the ultimate failure and was the lowest point in my life. Although I was eventually able to pick myself up and move on, I look back and realize that I robbed myself of that great experience both to overcome my fears and the opportunity to serve my country. I am certain that if my situation at home had been normal, this outcome would have been different. What a shame. To this day, it is of such profound regret to me that talking about it is still difficult. I did myself and my country a huge disservice, and it is a regret I continue to live with.

I was not in touch with my family during this period. An angry young man, I just wanted to strike out on my own. I doubt they would have approved of my life at that point either. However, after my discharge, my father, who had to come and sign me out, suggested I go to Sabta Edith in Basel. Not ready to make any decisions, I returned to bartending, but the effect on me of that failure was too great, and I became a creature of the night, aimlessly knocking around Tel Aviv, mixing with the wrong crowds and growing increasingly self-destructive. The only consistent interest that seemed to emerge was food. Boaz owned Yogi Deli in Tel Aviv; we talked a lot about the business, and I was intrigued and fascinated by his line of work. Boaz could see how frustrated I was and that I was heading nowhere. The truth was that now I felt trapped in Israel. Every time I went for a job interview, the first question would always be, 'What did you do in the army?' It was a terrible stain. Everyone is expected to do national service, no excuses. I could not look at myself in the mirror anymore. I was struggling to find an identity, an Israeli who had not done military service, has no real job, and little guidance from my family. Finally, Boaz, equally frustrated, told me to go to my grandmother in Switzerland because, as Boaz pointed out, I had always remained close to her, she had money, she was wise, and I desperately needed guidance and support.

I packed up and left Israel.

Chapter 4

The Iron Lady

My Sabta Edith was an exceedingly charismatic woman. Born in 1914, she became a ballerina, and as a young woman, she remained incredibly fit, hiking twenty to thirty kilometres daily without even breaking a sweat. We used to call her the Billy Goat because of the way she traversed the mountains of the Graubünden region of Switzerland. She was tiny but lean, muscular, and strong with a personality to match. Her blue eyes would penetrate you and rather than looking like a warm Jewish grandmother, she often looked quite formidable. Perhaps this had something to do with her background, having helped her husband, his four brothers, and her in-laws escape the Nazis during the Second World War.

We had kept in close touch over the years through correspondence and would meet when she visited Israel. So, when I landed at her doorstep 4,000 kilometres away in Basel, Switzerland, it took her just one look to see I was in need of love and guidance, and she immediately took charge. This was exactly what I needed. It was restorative for me to have someone take the time to care about my future. I had had little guidance from my parents, and with the academic difficulties I had faced, I had stopped believing in myself. My grandmother would imperceptibly plant seeds of confidence in me that would slowly grow and flourish during my time with her in Europe. She believed in me. Growing up, no one had believed in me, and, as a result, I had no faith in myself; no belief that I was capable of achieving anything. There was never any doubt in Sabta's mind that I could succeed. I would see it in the way she spoke to me, and it left me no room for self-doubt. Her drive and belief overpowered everything. A striking example of this was the way she had decided even before I arrived that she would enrol me back in a school. Many years later, I would meet my future wife Stephanie, another strong woman who showed profound faith in me. I am not ashamed to say that it was these women that gave me the vision to dream bigger.

* * *

Basel, Switzerland, was a quiet sleepy town located on the Rhine. Culturally, it was heavily Germanic with a touch of the Middle Ages about it. Like many of the historic cities in Europe, the rustic old architecture nestles harmoniously with the sleek modern buildings against a backdrop of the river. It was a picturesque and peaceful change after the difficulties I had left behind. Sabta Edith lived in an area known as Magnolia Park, which was very near the St Alban Church. She had split up with my grandfather Harry years earlier before I was born, after he had had an affair and then married his mistress. Such was her strength that she waited till the day her sons completed their national service to leave him. Sabta Edith's journey brought her to Basel after she met and married Dr Kurt Weil, a Swiss Jewish chemist. He was a voracious chain smoker with a huge sense of humour and lifelong limp, which he received after he was left incapacitated by a ski accident in Davos. We called him 'Gogo', and I slept in his study.

I was still quite an anxious young man, and to ease my loneliness, I would often listen to street musicians play. This led to my friendship with Guido, who was a guitar player. I had been introduced to music at a young age as my father was an avid guitar player himself and was in a band of his own. In my teenage years, I developed an obsession with Duran Duran, their lyrics resonated with me and continue to do so even today. Guido and I both loved music, and one of my enduring memories was when he invited me to join him for the Montreux Jazz festival. We drove across Switzerland in a vintage olive-green Volvo, which was as charming as the Black Afghani Hash we indulged in on the journey. There we rocked to my favourite Acta band featuring Manu Dibango; they had a terrific African funk-groove with songs like Soul Makossa. What a glorious trip! Music was my escape, and the energy of the people was infectious.

Meanwhile my grandmother was busy making plans for me. She firmly believed language was a powerful tool that would open up opportunities. Her first goal was for me to become fluent in German. She enlisted me into the Goethe Institute in nearby Freiburg, Germany, and with me in tow, she journeyed two hours north to meet the school's headmaster. At that meeting, she sternly told him that I was her grandson and that he better make sure I speak fluent German by the time she returned to pick me up in six months. The headmaster cowered, as many did in front of my grandmother, and he of course assured her that I would be fluent in six months. I also nodded furiously in compliance with the plan.

Ironically, I was much happier in Germany. I found myself living on a farm near the institute with an older couple as the commute from my grandmother's was too far. It was good for me to be independent. I enjoyed meeting international students from all over the world, and my friendships began to expand. There was Takasho, a Japanese race car driver, Pablo the musical conductor from Portugal, and Dunia from Catalonia. I was a naturally sociable person, and this felt like a new start for me. Academically, things were looking up. I made this wonderful discovery that I had a knack for languages, and it was fantastic because, for the first time, school was not a negative experience. Perhaps my grandmother saw this in me and that is why she sent me to the institute. I will never know if that was the case as I never had the chance to reminisce with her about this in later years.

Nevertheless, it turned out to be the right decision. It should have been strange; a young Jew, an Israeli, living in Germany. I expected all the history would make it difficult, but I actually felt very welcome. Germans are formal. They maintain that formality until they get to know you and trust you, so it is not easy making friends with them. But when you do, it's for life. Two of my closest friends today, Tobias and Kai, are both Germans I met during this period of my life. My grandmother was pleased with my progress as I did well at the institute, surely also to the headmaster's relief. Another huge plus was that commuting back and forth to the school in Freiburg, it became clear that I had hit a culinary jackpot. Baden-Baden is located in the Southwest region of Baden, Germany, which is in the largest of its thirteen wine appellations. It has the French border with Alsace, the Swiss border to its south, and Germany's warmest wine growing region, Kaiserstuhl, nearby. Throughout the Middle Ages, Alsace was a province of the Germanic Holy Roman Empire where wine growing dated back to the first millennium. The countryside was populated with beautiful vineyards growing mostly grapes for white wines such as Riesling, Pinot Blanc, and Pinot Gris. The nearby Black Forest—the actual forest, not the old-fashioned cake from the 1970s—was a charming and rustic place.

The University of Freiburg is a major landmark there and is world-famous. The area around it is well known for its cuckoo clocks and numerous microbreweries. There were many local farms with much of their tradition centred around food. Alsace boasts of its white asparagus, Black Forest ham, and wild game, and today its capital, Strasburg, teems with Michelin star restaurants. So, with all this around me, my culinary journey started to evolve. I began to taste the local wines, developed a real interest in them and learned how to pair wine with food. The cuisine was sophisticated and subtle, different from the earthy, more wholesome food I had grown up on. It was natural that I would gravitate back to what was familiar to me, what I had imbibed growing up, the one constant in my life: restaurants and hospitality. I found great comfort in the pleasure and sense of community that restaurants provided, and let's face it, I loved good food and wine even back then!

I began to sense that working in an industry that revolves around the culinary was perhaps where my future lay. Having grown up travelling and being exposed to both hotels and restaurants, hospitality was in my blood. My father had done culinary training, and I was smack in the middle of Baden-Baden, the prime region to pursue this career. After Goethe Institute, I would have to start making some decisions about my life, and I was starting to feel slightly more confident about doing so. I started researching hotel schools in Switzerland and Germany. I found the industry seductive with its opulence and the sense of adventure created by the comings and goings of sophisticated, world-class travellers. Hotels are the culmination of everything that is luxury under one roof. It has the allure of expensive brands, fine dining, cocktail bars, and service dispensed by immaculate, highly trained staff who take great pride in their work. Of course, the realities of regimented subservience and long hours did not figure in my still youthful

visions, but the pull of that world had been instilled in me
at a very young age. Or perhaps it was just the hope in the
air. It was 1990, the Berlin Wall had come down, and it was
an absolutely fascinating time to be in Germany. The words
of JFK echoed in my mind, 'ICH BIN EIN BERLINER'.
The Soviet Union was disintegrating, and there was a heady
euphoria with possibilities floating in the air. A new united
Germany and a united Europe. I was definitely carried forward
by that end-of-the-Cold-War optimism.

My grandmother, pragmatic as ever, was also thinking
of the next step for me and decided that I should become
a banker and there was discussion of going to America for
college. However, that did not appeal to me at all. I was not
ready to face America again and would not be for a long while.
Plus, Guy Wächs, the banker? It did not sound quite right. I
was now surer that I wanted to apply to hotel management
schools. Ecole hôtelière de Lausanne was and is the top hotel
school in the world. It was also unaffordable for us, or at least
my family was not willing to invest that sort of money in me,
given that I had such a poor academic record. There were
cheaper schools and I could easily have gone to one of those,
but they were second tier, and as far as I was concerned, I
only wanted to attend the best. I did have a stubbornness,
even back then, that belied my lack of confidence. I may not
always know what I want, but once I decide on it, I only want
the best. This trait of mine, never settling for anything less
than the best, has caused me difficulties but has also been
behind my successes.

In the meantime, this situation became quite a stalemate
between Sabta and me, and I asked my father for advice. So, he
flew to Germany to try and take things in hand. He arranged for
me to meet with Herr Von Koeller, the Regional Director at the
highly prestigious Steigenberger Europäischer Hof in Baden.

My father re-did my resume, asked me to put on my best suit, and told me I was going for a job interview in Baden-Baden. At a loose end, with no chance of getting hotel school funded, I went along. When the director of the hotel arrived to conduct the interview, he fulfilled all my fantasies about the hotel world. He was tall, very, very handsome and dressed to perfection. He looked like Harrison Ford, and I was charmed, but, of course, at the same time, severely intimidated as well. Fittingly, he was two hours late, and I of course waited patiently and gratefully. I was not fully prepared for what happened next. I was there for a *praktikum*, a short stint in a position to assess if it is the right vocation for the employee. As it turned out, they only had an opening in culinary, which was the one position I was absolutely not willing to do, but I could not express my views as I was busy sweating and stuttering like a nervous boy on a first date.

When I was crisply directed to the kitchen, I was flabbergasted. I protested that I had no clothes packed, was expected back at my grandmother's, and I still needed time to prepare myself mentally. My protestations were dismissed because it apparently had all been arranged with my father, and I was being put straight to work. This was the hotel world; it was authoritarian, hierarchical, and brutal. I was only there a week, but my dislike of the kitchen was confirmed. The work was intensely physical, and I was desperately unhappy. Yes, I loved the idea of working in an industry that revolved around high quality cuisine, but I was more interested in the hospitality aspect, not scrubbing floors.

I had held out against going to a second-tier hotel school and now foresaw years working in a kitchen. I was like a stricken, trapped animal, and it was apparent to the staff there. One of them mentioned that perhaps I would be happier at another hotel her boyfriend was doing his *praktikum* at because they had more opportunities outside of culinary, plus she told me that that hotel was the pinnacle of the industry for hotel diploma training. I went to check it out. Another route into hotel management is to do a Hotel Administration Diploma rather than a degree, which is obtained through a three-year apprenticeship. This costs nothing as the hotel looks after you while you live onsite and work for them. To me, this was preferable to going to a school which I did not consider was prestigious or good enough or being stuck in a job I disliked.

* * *

There have been many moments in my life where I think luck, or perhaps I would venture to say fate, has intervened. This was one of those times. I remember the moment I saw the Brenners Park-Hotel. As the property came into view, everything slowed down, the surroundings faded away, and there I was standing still, staring and smitten. When you approach the hotel, the nearby stream tinkles melodically and birds chirp, giving the hotel an ethereal quality. The classic nineteenth century structures incorporate a blend of understated modern architecture, old world without feeling old, and it transported me, in a profound way. The hotel echoed with fairy tales full of adventure and possibilities, and I desperately wanted to be part of that story. I could feel excitement and purpose, and my unfailing intuition told me this was where I belonged.

The question now was how could I get a *praktikum* at Brenners Park-Hotel? I knew that I was even willing to suffer a culinary position, if I could just join Brenners. Ironically, given the career I subsequently chose, culinary would have been the right place for me, but at that time, I had a strong aversion to kitchen work. The hotel world is small, and I was obliged by the privilege of having been given a *praktikum* at Steigneberger, to be grateful, and stay on. Perhaps, in hindsight, it was disrespectful or, at the very least, ungrateful, but once the week in the kitchen was over, I walked over to Brenners Park-Hotel, showed them my original acceptance letter from Stegneberger as leverage, and asked for a job. It was cheeky and perhaps I was still ignorant of the practices of this industry, but I would like to think it was my *chutzpah* asserting itself. I did not want to stay in culinary, I wanted to do hotel management, but most of all, I so very much wanted to work at Brenners Park-Hotel.

I managed to secure an interview but had to wait six months for it, and when I met William Luxem, the Hotel Manager, he glared at me and asked why he should consider me out of the two thousand applicants they get every year. I told him he should hire me because I was the best. My desperation had given me a new found confidence. Before any company decides to sponsor you for a three-year apprenticeship, they need to be very sure of you, and I was an unknown. They agreed to allow me to work for six months as a page boy, and if the head concierge was willing to recommend me after that, then, at that point, they would *consider* me. My father was a real asset when dealing with interviews and getting jobs. With his Paul Newman good looks, he was both elegant and charming, a winner when dealing with people. My father accompanied me to the interview, and I believe his presence made a big difference at the meeting, but still, I would have to prove myself during those six months to secure the *praktikum*.

So, I joined as an apprentice of Brenners Park-Hotel & Spa in Baden-Baden, Switzerland in 1991. The hotel was a charming old-world property set in the rustic Black Forest that till today remains an iconic feature of the area. It is famous for its horse racing, Casino Baden-Baden, and the Caracalla Spa named after the infamous and troubled Roman Emperor Caracalla, who, it is said, believed that the hot springs discovered 2,000 years earlier would keep him young forever. The springs, however, could not protect him against the ambitious army officer who assassinated him. For me, this hotel represented everything I desired: history, tradition, quality, and all the finer things in life that I knew existed and I very much wanted to be a part of.

The hours were very long and many, many a times I wanted to give up and walk away. The discipline at this academy was severe and I was terribly homesick. First, I would have to do my practical on the job training in the hotel and then attend the vocational hotel school for theoretical studies including business, maths, technology, and culinary studies. The last component would be the verbal and practical examination conducted by the Industrie und Handelskammer (trade ministry). Did I mention (a few times) that academics was not my strong point? It was grunt work. How to make a bed, clean a bathroom, shine windows and mirrors, wash dishes, cook food, serve food, and frappe a bottle of wine. Also, exchange foreign currency, send a fax, and type a menu. To survive and succeed, the hotel has to become part of your blood. You live and breathe the hotel, wear it on your uniform day in and day out, rain or shine, and as we learned, the hotel is you and you are the hotel. It consumes and takes over your life completely. You have no time for yourself, and this is a sacrifice you must make to survive this boot camp. I was determined, and with immense help from my classmates Tobias Busse and Kai Kenngott, I persevered and moved upwards.

Both Tobias and Kai were charming and dashing young men. Kai was my senior but generously took me under his wing, and I watched his energy and charm with the guests and learned. The image of him driving his navy-blue CTV Citroen convertible around Baden-Baden has remained entrenched in my memory. Today, he is the proud owner of Wine in the Hood in Wiess Baden. Tobias was my roommate and, being talented in hotel accounting, tutored me in math. He was important throughout my career, encouraging me not to give up when I was struggling in New York and even helping me get jobs. Today, Tobias works in asset management in New York City. Without these close bonds, it would have been even harder, and those friendships are more alive today than ever. We have witnessed each other's development as professionals, and we still speak weekly, even though we live on opposite sides of the world; I in Singapore, Kai in Wiess Baden, and Tobias in New York.

This was one of the most gruelling and perhaps most challenging experiences of my life. But, in many ways, I believe that this apprenticeship at Brenners Park-Hotel & Spa, was the making of me—the person and the restaurateur I would be in the future.

Chapter 5

The Apprentice

When you start anything in life, you are at the bottom of the pile. Still, I was at the bottom of the pile at a top hotel, so it was a fabulous place to start. The days began at 5 a.m. in pitch dark. Herr Troy, the chief concierge, ruled, and my first job was as an assistant under him. If by chance you happened to pass the hotel in the early 90s, you might have seen a skinny Jewish boy riding the hotel bicycle to the post office to collect the mail. I would deliver this to the concierge desk after which I would be sent up to collect guest shoes for polishing. On every floor, shoes placed in bags would be left hanging from door handles outside each room. I would gather them one by one and proceed to a little storeroom next to the service elevator where I would sit on a low stool and polish them vigorously for as long as was needed to get them shined to perfection. This meant waiting till I could see my reflection in them. After returning the shoes to the correct door handles, I would report back to Herr Troy.

By then, he would have sorted the morning post into piles for the guests and those for the different departments within the hotel. It was a comical ceremony involving a high degree of skill where each envelope was purposefully thrown like a stone skimming on water, sliding and jumping to accurately land on the correct pile for me to pick up and deliver to the different areas of the hotel. This ritual is one of the enduring memories I have of my internship and is indicative of the vitality of those individuals who worked in the hotel industry. In their many little ways, they drove the success of these grand hotels.

Herr Troy treated the job like military exercises, and everything had to be done with precision and discipline, or you risked incurring his wrath. He was so strict that he instilled the fear of God in me. The world of the concierge is prestigious, and they have a profound sense of pride in their profession. Concierges worldwide aspire to be a part of the esteemed elite association, Les Clefs d'Or. This is an invitation only group that is only extended to those whose reputations have put them at the top of their field, and they wear the key on their lapel as public recognition of this. It is not easy to be admitted to, and to carry the Golden Key Hotel Concierge is to be the ultimate insider. These concierges have the skills and the contacts to open doors that no others can, and "no" is not in their vocabulary. They have the most powerful people on their speed dial. Need a private jet to London? They can arrange it in an hour. Tickets to a sold-out opera in Rome? The answer is *yes*. You want to meet a porn star? No problem. The other concierges at Brenners Park were Herr Volmer, who was secretly the hotel detective and connected to the city police department (but no one was supposed to know), and the third, Senior Morretti, was all Italian charm, but unfortunately not blessed with good looks. The Three Musketeers of Brenners Park-Hotel, they all carried the Golden Keys proudly on their white jackets. They were the ring masters.

Roll call was a unique experience. I would stand in front of Herr Troy at 7 a.m., nervous and ready for inspection. It all had to be perfect; from my socks, shoes, and buttons to the quality of my shave and the length of my nails. I had to wear crisp white clean gloves, and if anything was wrong, I would be sent back to my room to straighten out the offending item and report back. In hotel training, you are required to do it all. I licked hundreds of stamps, placing them meticulously on the corner of the envelopes until the taste of glue remained with me for years. I polished all the brass fixtures and cleaned the many, many windows. Many years later, I realized that hotel management was not my calling, but as a hotel intern, I would spend a lot of time in departments like stewarding, housekeeping, service, pantry, reception, and banqueting. Of course, ultimately, none of this experience was wasted, but at that time, I ended up struggling. I was never good with numbers and consistently had problems working at the front office because of the accounting involved. I would get terribly frustrated as my dyslexia meant that I would switch numbers and get confused. It was not the right place for me, and if I had realized earlier that this was not the place for me, it would have saved me a lot of career hopping. That is not to say those early years did not give me—albeit many years later—so many of the skills it took to open a restaurant of my own.

Banquet service for big events, I learned the hard way, was about synchronization, dramatic execution, and perfect timing. My first experience as a server went very badly. The venue was the Riders Club of Baden-Baden, and the guest of honour was the famous American politician and diplomat, Henry Kissinger and his wife Nancy. Upon picking up the appetizers from the kitchen, I enthusiastically strode out to serve Mrs Kissinger, but to my horror, I suddenly realized that I was the lone server in a large dining room with hundreds of people. I had forgotten the cardinal rule of serving, which was to wait to get permission from the head waiter. I ran back into the kitchen, and with all eyes on me, I was forced to return the soup. To say I felt terrible would be an understatement. Mr Lebak nearly killed me, and I was awash with shame and embarrassment. I spent the rest of the night polishing the floor for my transgression and thereafter was known as the 'waxer'. Banquet service is based on military precision. I never made that mistake again, and it taught me the importance of following instructions and being a good listener.

Apart from the inevitable hiccups on the job, it was also gruelling work, seven days a week with no rest during the peak holiday periods. It got so demanding at times that one December, we worked for twenty-four hours straight, and the next morning when I collapsed on my bed and took off my shoes, I realized to my dismay that my toenails were bleeding. This was just one of the many horror stories of working in the industry.

* * *

The maître d' of the hotel, Mr Martin Lebek, became my first mentor. Before joining Brenners Park-Hotel, Mr Lebek worked in the cruise industry on the 5-star luxury liner, M.S. Europa, sailing around the world, where it was normal to work for blocks of six months without any days off. Imagine feeding 500 passengers three times a day, every day, only to begin again the next day. At the height of his career in 1993, he received the head waiter of the year award from the prestigious Gaullt Milau guide. I lived in fear of him. Still, I understood the value of overcoming my fear and learning from his vast wealth of experience. I still visit Martin every time I am in Baden-Baden, and we have become good friends.

At Brenners Park-Hotel & Spa, we were drilled on being ready 24/7, we were not expected or even permitted to depart from the established standard operating procedures, or as the industry knows them, the SOP of the hotel. Our work was repetitive and boring, trudging through the menial tasks of cleaning, mopping, schlepping, and we had no idea why we needed to do these jobs. What exactly was it teaching us? However, we also had to develop our awareness to notice small details that did make a big difference. We would never enter a guest room without knocking; if a guest arrived at the hotel, we opened the car door, assisted with the luggage, checked in the guest, and escorted them to their room. Was the room at the correct temperature? Was the safe deposit box working? Was there an umbrella in the closet? Did the guest want to pre-order their breakfast for the next day? Did they need the morning paper in English, French, or German? Did they require theatre tickets or a spa treatment? Our duty was to connect all the dots and make everything happen in the best possible way and above all, anticipate their needs, even before they knew they had them.

Becoming a hotelier required both human and technical skills, and at the time, I had no idea of the value of repetitive work. Three years of apprenticeship in a hotel was like taking a deep breath in, and three years later, a deep breath out. Cooking: I was cutting, dicing slicing, cleaning, and freezing. Stewarding: Scrubbing from top to bottom. Then do it again, and again, and again. Serving: Serve from the right, clear from the left; clear with your thumb on the fork; food debris onto the base plate; carry plates in your left hand, clear with your right. Cellaring: collect bottles, receive stock, restock, update wine list. Housekeeping: Dusting and vacuuming. Bed-making. Washing the bathroom, first the showers, then the baths, then the sinks, and then the mirrors. As concierge: do it all. Note everything, tick off what is done, follow every safety rule or risk wrath. Boring repetitive tasks. But slowly, my focus began to change from frustration and exhaustion to becoming an expert. This experience became the grounding philosophy many years later at the restaurant I would open in Singapore in 2009, Wild Honey. All this is collectively known as the 5 Ps: Presentable, Punctual/Present, Personable, Positive Attitude, and Product knowledge.

This was an industry that often catered to the high-end establishment. I was meeting the who's who and had some wild experiences. We became experts in the art of discretion, which was essential as we met many celebrities. Whether escorting dignitaries or envelopes of cash, no questions can be asked in this business. Gossiping about our guests was considered to be extremely bad form. I began to love every single part of that magnificent, enchanting castle and became intimate with all the areas of the hotel. In many ways, we were sheltered from the outside world as any mistake by us would be at the expense of the hotel. Speaking of mistakes, I got lazy one day and used the public guest bathroom in the hotel. When my beloved General Manager Mr. Richard Schmitz noticed, he said, "I see our staff bathroom is not good enough for Mr Wächs." I nearly died of embarrassment, and yes, I never made that mistake again. Once during breakfast, I asked our guest, the famous rock singer Lou Reed, for his autograph. I forgot to respect his space, and he was furious at me. I learned to respect people's privacy the hard way, through mistakes.

One of my favourite guests was the indomitable Joan Collins, a.k.a. the Denver Beast. Anyone who grew up in the 80s would recognize the dazzling star of the famous Hollywood soap opera *Dynasty*. She was charming and spirited, and I treasured meeting such interesting people. She was staying at the hotel during the filming of an episode of *Dynasty* when a fire broke out in the Residence Turgenjew, a building directly across from the hotel. She was the first to notice it and took charge straight away, quickly instructing her crew and me (who was nearby) to attend to the fire. Luckily, we were able to successfully evacuate two elderly guests. She and I made a great team. Ms Collins barking instructions at me and me running like crazy to help. With Ms Collins demanding I take action, I climbed up onto the second floor despite my fear of heights and threw myself in, more terrified of her than the fire. My little amateur heroics managed to impress Ms Joan Collins herself!

One day, I even got to star in a small international intrigue. One of my favourite jobs at the hotel was chauffeuring as I got to drive the hotel limousine to the airport in Frankfurt and back. I was a young man driving a nice car in a city with no speed limit on the highway. What was there not to like? I started doing some driving on the side for extra money, and one day Herr Troy asked me to do a hush hush job, as he put it. Nothing like a bit of mystery to spice things up. My destination was a large hangar in a huge industrial complex. No information was given to me at the time. I was just told to drive there alone and await further instructions.

As I drove to the destination, I wondered what was up and thought perhaps it was a famous but discreet actor or model that needed transport. It turned out to be much more dramatic than that. When I arrived in Stuttgart, in the middle of the industrial hangar stood ten identical white Mercedes Benz, all lined up with German flags on their bonnets, accompanied by flags of white, blue, and red that were completely unfamiliar to me. The unfamiliar flags were Russian and the cars were being used for a state visit of the then Russian President, Boris Yeltsin. Our job was to pick him up from the airport and drive him to the Mercedes Benz factory and then onwards to his hotel. I was in the convoy driving the President of Russia around! I had no passengers myself and had to drive the last car, which was used to make sure no other cars entered the convoy of Mercedes. I weaved left from right to left to right, keeping other cars from entering our convoy. What a thrill! This was one of the most enjoyable times of my life.

I graduated from Brenners Park-Hotel in 1993. German unification was no longer news, the internet was yet to become widespread, and it would be another year before the Netscape web browser would be released. I was on top of the world. Thinking that I had arrived at my destination, I looked forward to bee lining into management. This was characteristically naïve of me and, like everyone else, I had to start at the bottom again. I made the wrong decision and decided to focus my career on the rooms division and got my first job as a guest service agent at the reception of the Hotel Zurich.

My strength has always been, and still is, in guest relations skills. One thing my father taught me very well was the art of improvization. Imagine you have one hundred guest rooms, and a flight arrives with a hundred and ten guests. How do you find ten additional rooms? What happens if you have a company dinner party for five hundred with white wine as an aperitif and suddenly the Japanese CEO changes his mind and switches his preference to beer? How do you find five hundred beer glasses on the fly? It is the US Open tennis event, and the restaurant toilet gets clogged up. How do you fix that? Learning to handle the unexpected is critical for any leader, and this was clearly my strength. I proved to be very useful with demanding guests.

I remember a long-staying elderly guest in the hotel got highly agitated when we removed a painting from her room to be cleaned. Immediately, the staff called for me as they knew I had a good relationship with her and would calm her down. I had a knack for knowing when to be gentle, when to flatter, and when to be firm, and it was a skill that helped me through many difficult situations. I was able to think quickly on my feet. At the same time, I also realized my weaknesses, such as, that the front office was a disaster for me. Front office requires a good foundation in numbers and still not aware of my dyslexia, my many mistakes frustrated me. My biggest mistake though was not owning up to my shortcomings. When confronted by my supervisors, I would become defensive and angry, and in the end, this did not help my career. Not only did it hinder my progress, but my self-confidence took some hard knocks. I was frustrated at not being able to use my creative side and found corporate politics hard to navigate. I was never good at being a team player, and this was a big factor in motivating me to start my own business fifteen years later.

* * *

It was 1995, and I had now been away for four years and began to miss home and at the same time felt the need for a change professionally as I was getting increasingly frustrated with the work I was doing. After returning, I got a job with Isrotel, a local hotel group, at their Royal Beach Hotel in Eilat. It was a beautiful 5-star property located directly on the Red Sea, where every guest room had an ocean view. I started as a Guest Service Agent or GSA, then was promoted to shift leader, and thereafter as assistant manager, where I also functioned as their night manager for a year.

I was able to use many of the skills I had learned in Europe. One of the problems in this hotel was drunk gambling guests who played at the Hilton Hotel casino nearby in Taba, which was over the border on the Egyptian side. They could become violent when they lost money and smash things, including occasionally my face. It was here I met my second mentor, Nur Amar, an Israeli Druz. He was a great role model for me. He was loved by his team, and his charm and wit impressed everyone. He always had my back, and I will never forget him. He was an extremely strong leader, and from the moment I met him, I decided I wanted to be like him. My admiration for him became even more pronounced when he rescued me from what could have become a career changing incident.

The high rollers at the casino who stayed in the hotel would often pay in cash, and one day, we had a payment of $25,000 in cash. The procedure was that after the shift, the cash is taken to the back office where we count the money and then deposit it in the safe. Needing a quick bathroom break, I left the money unattended for just half a minute. When I came back, it was apparent a large chunk of that money was gone. I was devastated and kept wondering if I had made a counting error rather than the sickening feeling that someone had taken it. $10,000 was missing, and I was beside myself. Nur calmly told me to go home and told me that he would handle it.

A week later, he called me into his office and asked me to close the door. I thought that was it, I was going to lose my job and get reported to the police. Nur asked me gently if I had taken it, and I vehemently denied it, saying I was even willing to take a lie detector test. Nur believed me and made the problem go 'away' by accounting for the discrepancy through discounts on the rooms. This was a huge thing to do and showed what kind of a leader he was. Thank you, Nur!

I was equally impressed by the owner of the hotel, the South African Mr David Lewis, and learned many important lessons from him. One of these was that he would always check in and stay in room 401. Room 401 was the only room in the entire hotel where the view was obstructed by the hotel restaurant. I was dumbstruck. Why would the owner stay in the worst room? Nur explained to me that David wanted to know what it would be like as a guest in the worst room. What commitment to his craft! He was not interested in the trappings of success but instead dedicated himself to the service of the country, opening several 5-star hotels in the region to help develop the area. He dressed like an old uncle; he wore sandals, shorts, and a short sleeve shirt to stay incognito. He wanted to see how his staff would interact with an average person. These were valuable lessons to be learned from successful business owners.

The isolation of working in the desert was compensated for by the beauty of the Sinai and the opportunity to scuba dive in the famous Red Sea with its variety of colourful coral and abundance of hammerhead sharks. It was also good to be near my parents again and this also became a hiatus from the difficulties we had experienced together in the past. But Eilat, as idyllic as it was, was still a resort town. For a young man, it was too small. Besides, I had done two years in Eilat, and cabin fever was starting to really show. By this time, my fear of the US had also passed, and, in fact, I had become very much aware that it was a land of opportunities. I needed to get out of hotels and into the restaurant business, and the USA seemed the right place for that shift. Coincidentally, my brother was about to graduate from college, and my parents asked me to accompany them there.

Twenty-four years after my father went to American to pursue his dream, I followed in his footsteps. Would it be different for me?

Chapter 6

Journeyman

Arriving in New York City in 1997 was amazing, and I felt tiny in the big city. We attended my brother Daniel's graduation from the Curtis Institute of Music in Philadelphia and after the graduation ceremony, they travelled back to New York with me, and we stayed in Central Park South in a historic but by now dump of a hotel, The St Moritz (incidentally where Duran Duran stayed on their US tour). I remember odd details about that time, like not having enough warm clothes, my parents taking me to Carnegie's Deli for my first glorious Reuben sandwich, and being hit on by an attractive middle-aged woman at the Plaza Hotel Bar. This last incident amused my father to no end. 'Welcome to New York City,' he said to me.

In the late 90s, the hotel industry was booming in the city, and this was the place to break into the job market. Through my good old friend Tobias Busse, I was offered the position of assistant manager at the Mark Hotel. Unfortunately, I failed their drug test (I promise, like Bill Clinton, I smoked, but I never inhaled). Does it really take two weeks to get marijuana out of your body? Anyway, obviously I did not get that job. I eventually found work as a guest services agent at the Crowne Plaza on Times Square.

Accommodation proved tricky. The city is expensive for a young person starting out, but my good friend Barry Meyer, whom I knew from nightlife in Israel, was kind enough to let me sleep on his sofa. I was determined to change things by staying clean and keeping away from drugs. The flat comprised a hotchpotch of people. Barry was studying fashion at the Fashion Institute of Technology and dreamed of becoming a designer. He shared his loft on Gansevoort Street, a gritty area in the meatpacking district a stone's throw from the West Village, with a Russian model, of course named Olga. She was a hand and foot model and used to party with UV lights and techno music blaring in the room she shared with her daughter. Cool looking young boys from the hood would turn up, and it was all wild partying to techno music. I could not connect to that scene. I was broke with no credit card from mommy and daddy, and when I tried to open a checking account at Citibank, they required a minimum deposit of $2,000, which I did not have. Luckily Republic Bank was kinder to me, so I at least obtained a debit card, but I had to get out of that accommodation before I got sucked into that life. So, I went from one friend's sofa bed to the next, and it took me a long time to settle down in NYC. One kind soul who took pity on me was my grandmother's cousin, Ilse Freidenberg, who was a piano teacher. She was an extremely elegant silver haired lady who looked out for me and encouraged me to work hard and remain humble. 'You will become successful,' she would promise me whenever I visited her in her home near Lincoln Centre on the Upper West Side. Significantly, she invited me for lunch one day with her son Peter Friedenberg at Café Luxembourg on the Upper West Side, where I would later get a job. A very cool place for an old lady to take a young man for lunch. She had class.

Looking back, without people like Barry, Ilse, and Tobias, I would not have lasted one month in the city. It was people like them who, apart from the help with jobs, accommodation, and hospitality, kept me grounded in the big and lonely city. The cold weather was debilitating and living out of a suitcase was a challenge. After a whole year of living and working at night and sleeping during the day, I started to feel like a vampire.

On the career front, this nomadic life was paying off though because I was making a good name for myself in the hotel. The guests seemed to love me, and I was quickly promoted to night manager. Working in Times Square was exciting as it was at the centre of New York and very happening. The expense accounts that people had to pay for rooms and meals at the hotel amazed me, and this was despite having worked in a hotel near the casino in Israel.

The yield manager was a young Israeli man who was very aggressive with overbooking the hotel's 770 rooms. So, it actually became 770 plus another twenty as he would always double book twenty rooms. On top of that, he also used airline rooms as double occupancy to increase revenue. Good trick. When things got hairy, we would walk the guest to the Marriott Marquis next door to get a room there. High stakes, high tension! This was real on the job experience, and, in New York, there were no second chances, or you would get replaced in a flash. This was invaluable to my progress. As the Chairman (Frank Sinatra) once said about New York, 'If I make it there, I'll make it anywhere.'

I will never forget the New Year's Eve as we saw in the new millennium. It was 31 December 1999, and we thought that all the clocks would stop working and the elevators in the hotel would come to a standstill. At least that was what the news cycles were telling us day in and day out. Times Square was having the countdown with thousands of people, and the whole area was cordoned off. We were expecting our VIP Grace Jones to arrive, but we were informed she needed assistance both for reaching the hotel and for getting to her concert on time. She was severely delayed, and I found her with her son and driver in their car a few blocks away from the hotel, stuck in massive traffic blocked by the throngs of people. We transferred all her luggage onto the hotel trolley, and I pushed it through the streets back to the hotel, weaving through cars and crowds. Then I raced her across for her show at Studio 54. After her concert, she invited me to her room to 'fix the fax machine'. The fax machine, of course, was not broken. I should have gone! Duty came first, and I did not (plus I was shy).

I found some stability finally when I found a gem of a studio apartment on the Upper East Side on 85th Street which became my sanctuary. Life in hotels is an endless cycle of shifts and working long nights, but finally I could just go home and crash in my own space.

Still, I could not shake that feeling that I was somehow not in the right place. I wanted to move up to a more senior position in the hotel; I was frustrated and felt under-appreciated. I was outspoken which was not liked by management, and I had very few friends and no social life because of my long hours at work. By 2000, it became clear to me that my career in hotels was not progressing as I had hoped. I knew that I needed to leave the familiar and safe environment of hotels and take a jump into the unknown.

In hotels, you are just a part of a big organization, and your footprint is limited. I was looking for more control and autonomy, somewhere I felt, where I could be seen and would have freedom to be myself. Besides, in a hotel, you are answerable to each department head, often each with their own agenda. I am not good with even one boss let alone many! I felt restaurants were the right direction for me to move into. In a restaurant, I would be free to assert my personality. Hospitality is a creative art, and I was ready to explore my own interpretation of that art.

* * *

After seeing an advertisement in the *New York Times*, I applied for a position at Cafe Luxembourg, and my friend Guy Heksch, the General Manager of DB Bistro, gave me a personal recommendation. The cafe was owned by Lynn Wagenknecht, the ex-wife of restauranteur and celebrity Keith McNally who was behind some of New York's most popular institutions including Balthazar, Odeon, Nell's, Lucky Strike, and Pastis. The menu was Paris bistro fare and, I have to say, included the best steak frites in the city.

I was interviewed by the iconic restaurateur, Susan Kaufman, the woman behind the award-winning restaurants Serafina and Cicchetti. She was a real old school pro who had worked under the legendary restaurateur Danny Meyer who, years later, would write *Setting the Table*, a book that speaks to my creative and ambitious side and has strongly influenced my approach to running a successful restaurant. Susan immediately recognized the value of my European training and hired me as a maître d'. We got along very well, and when she was later dismissed, I could never really see eye to eye with the new boss. Until she left, I had the privilege to be personally trained by Susan.

Working the door at Cafe Luxembourg was extremely challenging as we needed to seat three separate groups every night. Pre-theatre, prime-time, and post-theatre. Each group had two hours for their dinner, and meals needed to be served and completed with precision to keep the show on the road! The late-night bar became very loud, and some mischievous guests found the basement where the staff locker room and prep kitchen were situated. They decided that it would be ideal for their 'after hour activities'. That's New York for you. The location of the cafe on West 7th Street put it near the iconic Lincoln Center, and this proximity to the arts centre was one of the reasons for its popularity. I had the pleasure of serving many local celebs from the Upper West Side including Yoko Ono, Cindy Lauper, Bono, and the most handsome couple in the world—Michael Douglas and Catherine Zeta-Jones. I also served Robert De Nero, Harrison Ford, Marianne Faithfull, Al Pacino, and my favourite, the great Donald Sutherland.

This break into the restaurant world proved invaluable to me. Not being good in a corporate environment, I definitely felt more comfortable working in this kind of small unit having just one boss. More importantly, it gave me a chance to hone the skills that I really needed. Becoming a certified sommelier was now something I understood and valued the importance of. I dressed better, spoke better, and my time keeping was fine tuned. All in all, it was a maturing experience for me, and by the end of it, I could honestly say I had learned to become a host rather than just a waiter. My comfort in small units was a defining factor and would profoundly influence the decisions I made in Singapore years later.

The late hours at Café Luxembourg were not suiting me, so having again responded to a *New York Times* ad, I moved on to Cafe Centro in 2001 as their restaurant manager. My Swiss boss Peter Wyss was a fantastic mentor, and he had an impressive work ethic. He would walk around the MetLife building on Park Avenue every morning and greet everyone by name, keeping us all on our toes. This left a huge impression on me: do not build walls between your staff and you. At Café Centro, I learned another important skill for running a business and that was cost control. I was in charge of managing the food cost and paying suppliers, and this helped me better understand the connection between buying supplies and turning them into saleable goods. This required keeping detailed records of inventory and procurement, which are critical steps for any restaurant worth its salt. A chef may have many gifts, but if they lack a strong business foundation, it can be the downfall of a restaurant.

My job was to work with the executive chef to ensure his blood, sweat and tears resulted in financial success, which meant that the link between purchasing, preparing, execution, menu design, sales, and accounting needed to be managed in detail. That can be very difficult considering that it is a constantly moving target; so whenever possible, I searched for new technology to help me. The introduction of Google Docs was a huge breakthrough as the sharing of information improved productivity. I also became very fluent with Oracle's Micros/Fidelio Point of Sales software. Restaurants have become huge investments and this experience in the enterprise of restaurants was critical for my future. I love and understand good food; I am not a good cook but I do however know how to turn a profit while still providing quality.

In addition, while at Café Centro, I got the opportunity to experiment with my creative side. Having cut my teeth in the hotel business, I understood the connection between hotels and other businesses, and in an effort to increase our customer base, I developed a concierge loyalty programme where we paid hotel concierges to recommend our café to their hotel guests. The vice president of the restaurant group loved it, and I received the Compass Group award for this programme. It increased revenues, and for me, it felt great to be recognized for my business instinct. This would influence my strategy in building a regular client base in my future projects. I would always focus on long-term relationships.

Around this time, the tech revolution in restaurants took off, and we began to use the OpenTable reservation system. Previously, we had relied on the good old pen and paper to keep records of our diners. It worked, but the new technology now made it possible to up this to another level. We could now track guest behaviour like favourite dishes, preferred payment mode, birthdays, and favourite tables. Information was fast becoming a commodity, and I made it a priority to remember guest names by giving them nicknames, and wherever possible, I would add their photos to our records.

By this time, Café Centro was a well-known, well-oiled machine with 400 seats, an 80-seater beer garden, and an outdoor standing bar. Situated behind Grand Central station, it was a real cash cow.

My future wife Stephanie was a regular guest at the café, together with her boss Bob Jeffrey, who was the CEO of JWT advertising agency. Being located near Madison Avenue, the heart of the advertising world, we had many 'Mad Men' with big expense accounts who would visit us.

One particular regular, Mr. Richards, would enter at 12 noon sharp like clockwork and in his heavy New England accent greet me, 'Good afternoon, Guy, how are you?' He was always dressed to kill in a perfectly tailored Tom Ford suit, a matching handkerchief in his breast pocket, silver hair gelled back, and a Rolex watch to complete the look. The moment he was seated, his extra dry martini would be served, and he would open his *Wall Street Journal*. Lunch was always the same. He began with a seafood salad and another martini. For main; the fresh scallops from Long Island on a bed of mashed yams. Dessert was key lime pie with a double espresso. In my two years of serving him, I never gave him a menu. What for? I knew everything he needed. It is helpful in hospitality to be observant and curious about people. You never know what you

will learn next. For my efforts, every Christmas Mr. Richards
gifted me a very generous envelope to express his thanks.

It is not just customers you need to look out for; restaurant
critics also frequent popular establishments, and they can make
or break us. I had a picture of the restaurant critic William
Grimms from the *New York Times* on me at all times in case he
turned up. I also kept a look out for Tim and Nina Zagat, who
published the most influential restaurant guide in the city, *The
Zagat Guide*. People skills and curiosity are very useful in this
business.

Service is incredibly physical work, and I was working over
sixty hours a week, but what I loved about New York was that
everyone helped everyone else. It was teamwork! Sometimes,
when we ran out of fresh lobsters, my head chef, Frank Delatrain,
would send me downstairs to the Grand Central Oyster Bar
Restaurant to get some. There was a sense of camaraderie and
cooperation amongst restaurateurs because we all belonged to
the same club. It was a club that provided us with a gruelling,
tumultuous, and exhausting adventure where you were always
on your feet. One trick I learned from the legendary head waiter
from Peter Luger, Mr. Wolfgang, was to change shoes and
socks twice a day. Good simple advice for tired feet. Years later,
Mr Wolfgang opened a restaurant in Singapore too!

My personal life also took an about turn during this period
because I met Stephanie, and that just changed everything. If
I had not met Stephanie, then perhaps I would have just kept
going in circles, one job to the next, with none really giving
me the opportunity to explore my own talent and creativity.
Clichéd as it may sound, I felt like a singer-songwriter who
was waiting to be discovered, because I could never shake the
feeling that there was something more waiting for me. It was
meeting Stephanie that would change that. She would give me
the confidence to stay in restaurants because, like my Sabta, she

had this tremendous faith in me. From the outset, from the way Stephanie looked at me, I could see her fundamental belief in me, which gave me the confidence I was often lacking.

* * *

Stephanie and I met in 2000 at a bar called the Le Bateau Ivres. I had been dating an Austrian girl who was far too young for me, and she had been dating a French boy who was far too young for her. We had both just been dumped by these youngsters and we both happened to be out commiserating at the same bar at the same time with our friends. Towards the end of the evening, as our friends slowly drifted off, we ended up chatting. Although we were very different—Stephanie was a vice-president, a power career woman, and I was just this run-of-the-mill restaurant manager—we also had things in common. We were both strangers in New York, we both loved wine and food, and we were both kind of on this big adventure far from our homes and families and had come to the city to make it big. In that sense, we were kindred spirits. I dropped her off, but of course wanted to stay in touch, so we exchanged numbers.

Now, fate played its hand. That first meeting with Stephanie took place the night before I started my job at Café Luxembourg. The next morning, the first day at the new job, perhaps because of nerves, I left my phone in the taxi on the way to work. Stephanie's number was on that phone, and without it, I had no way of contacting her. I resigned myself to never seeing her again, and this put a damper on that first morning at work because meeting Stephanie had been such a tremendous experience. Knowing New York City, there was little prospect of ever recovering my phone. Well, believe it or not, the unthinkable happened, and a couple who got in the taxi right after me found my phone and brought it to the cafe to give it back to me. This was unheard of in the Big Apple. In Singapore, yes, that may happen, but in New York City? When I got my phone back, there was a voice message from Stephanie, wishing me good luck at my new job. If that phone had not been returned, I would never have heard that sweet and thoughtful message. I knew then and there what a special person she was and that I had to ask her out on a proper first date.

At that time, I was living in a small studio on the Upper East Side on 86th and First in Little Germany, and my father happened to be visiting from overseas. On the night that I was supposed to take Stephanie on our first date, he left the house without a key. Of course, that meant that I could not lock the apartment and go out. So, I had no choice. I called Stephanie and told her what clearly sounded like an improbable story. She predictably did not believe it and told me in no uncertain terms that it was a really lame excuse to get out of a date. Stephanie is from Australia, and she does not mince her words. 'On the contrary, our date is very much on,' I told her. 'Please take a taxi. Here's my address, and I'll cook you dinner.' She came along to my studio, I cooked some pasta with a cream sauce, and then my father of course walked smack into the middle of my date and sat down to join us for dinner. So, there we were, Stephanie, my father, and I cozy on my first date with my future wife. When I kissed her goodbye before she got in her taxi, I knew she was the one.

We married on 28 September 2001, six months after meeting and two weeks after 9/11.

Chapter 7

Stephanie

Stephanie infected me with the love for all that is food, and to this day, even as the partner of a successful restaurant; she is still hands down my favourite cook. Stephanie, like Sabta Edith, is pivotal in my life. Her warmth and belief in me gave me confidence and allowed me to take the risks that are needed to become a successful entrepreneur. Moreover, Stephanie was integral to the success of Wild Honey in her own right. The Yin to my Yang, she balanced all the areas I struggled in, and the team that emerged both in our business partnership and our marriage has brought me the most profound joy. However, it was an unlikely connection, given how very different Stephanie's background was to mine.

Growing up in the suburbs of Sydney, Stephanie could never have imagined she would one day live and work in New York or spend the vast majority of her adulthood working outside of Australia, travelling and living all over. Little did she know that her childhood dream of owning a restaurant would also come to fruition after quitting her life in advertising. Once she traded her platinum travel card for an apron, she never looked back.

* * *

Her childhood in Australia could not have been more different from mine; she describes it as a very middle-class suburban family life. She has an older sister and a younger brother; her mother was her father's second wife. Her father was from a different generation and then some more, being twenty-two years my mother-in-law Judith's senior.

In my family, I had always felt life was like being thrown in the deep end of a pool without having been given swimming lessons. It was only after meeting Stephanie that these aspects of my childhood became clearer to me.

Learning about her life; I realized I did not have the guardrails, the direction, or the mentorship from my family. For some reason, despite my lack of direction or confidence, Stephanie really believed in me and saw my potential.

Steph enjoyed growing up in the eastern suburbs of Sydney with its beautiful beaches and immense views. As youngsters, Stephanie and her siblings would meet up with their best friends, leaving the house in the morning to disappear for hours; very often lured by the danger and thrill of scaling the cliffs facing the ocean and spending hours down there exploring the caves. She and her siblings learned to sail in the tiny nine-foot Sabots at the Vaucluse Amateur Sailing Club. They would race most Sundays in the summer and autumn on Sydney Harbour in and amongst the lightning fast eighteen footers and the slower but hugely daunting oil tankers that made their way up and down the channels in the harbour. They were not the best of sailors but did manage to bring home a few trophies over the years.

Stephanie had several Jewish friends and later on even dated some Jewish boys. She was always fascinated with the eating rituals and foods of Passover and Rosha Shona and developed a taste for matzo ball soup which she would eat with gusto at 21 in Double Bay on a Sunday night along with the tyre sized plates of chicken schnitzel and creamed spinach. These were all

very valuable experiences and a fantastic precursor to meeting
me, I like to think.

While Stephanie enjoyed school—quite different to my
experience—her mother and grandparents were outstanding at
science and maths, and she was a little embarrassed that she
did not take to these subjects at all. She naturally gravitated
towards reading and languages and that was where her talents
lay. She spent hours at art galleries and got to know the different
artists, styles, and periods and particularly loved many of the
early Australian artists and their work. Her love of the arts and
natural creativity is reflected in her flair for the beautiful and
the unique, and without this, the whole vision of Wild Honey
would not have materialized.

A love of literature and art was not, however, going to
build a career. Did I mention her pragmatic side? When she
left school; the economy was not great, and she decided to
study commerce, thinking she would become an accountant. I
cannot see that in her at all, and even though she is good with
numbers and business, the boredom of accountancy would
have done her in. She obviously realized this and changed her
major to marketing and it is in this field where her immediate
future and talents lay.

While at the UNSW, she was lucky enough to have
been offered an internship with Sudler & Hennessey, a
pharmaceutical advertising agency on the North Shore. It was
here that she got a taste for the creative business of advertising
and its varied and fascinating people. As it would turn out, this
was more than fortuitous as the connections she made paved
the way for her early advertising career. While never planned, it
seemed to Steph that one door opened, then another, and then
yet another, and it was just kismet.

Armed with a B.Com., she landed her first real job with
market research giant A.C. Nielsen, which was ironic as it

was a quantitative market research company, and by her own admission, she was terrible at maths. She worked diligently and ended up as an account manager on some powerhouse accounts like McWilliams Wines and Boots Pharmaceuticals, but Kellogg was her largest and most prestigious client.

Eventually, the Marketing Director of Kellogg had a word with JWT (J. Walter Thompson) and voila her first stint at JWT Healthcare emerged as did the beginning of her on-again off-again relationship with JWT and Kellogg. After a few years at boutique creative agency Forbes Macfie Hansen, she moved back to JWT to run the Kellogg business in Sydney, which proved to be the biggest turning point of her life. Through this work she was recruited to head the troubled Kellogg business at JWT Toronto, and after several years in Canada, she moved to Chicago to head the KRAFT USA business, followed by many happy years at JWT New York running Unilever.

If this was not a quality pedigree towards understanding the making of brands and the sheer power of great brands, I am not sure what would be.

* * *

Working and living in NYC was a dream. And a big one at that. The first time Stephanie had been to NYC, it was to interview for the role of Director in Charge for Kellogg Canada. She had travelled a bit—around Australia, to Fiji, and a big trip to Europe cycling around France—and then she got the call from Chris Jones, the global CEO of Kellogg at that time, to ask her if she would like to interview with them in Australia or in New York. It was no contest, and pretty soon she was jetting off to New York. She loves recounting that the first stop she made when she unloaded her bags at the hotel was to head off to Dean and Deluca on the corner of Prince and Broadway and got a kick out of the cab driver, who swore when they got chatting that she was a native New Yorker, and he took some convincing that she was just a girl from Sydney. She just loved the buzzing food mecca with its incredible, large floor-to-ceiling glass windows and espresso bar facing Broadway, the fantastical cheese displays, fresh flowers, bread, meats, charcuteries, and French porcelain homewares. At the time, there really was not anything like it back in Australia.

She fell in love with New York and its incredible energy with talent oozing out of every pore but unfortunately had to wait a few years until she would live there as it was off to Toronto first to save the Kellogg business.

Once she got back to Australia, she had just about three weeks to pack up and leave the only home she had ever known. She was single with not much in the way of worldly possessions. As she describes it, she just raced through it—packed her clothes, books—including all her cookbooks—and some art to take with her, offloaded her plants, BBQ, iron and ironing board, sold the rest, and got on that long flight with the bare necessities.

The job was intense but lucrative, and she flourished in the challenging environment of a client–agency relationship on the brink, and over time, she was able to prove herself to her many bosses, colleagues and clients, many of whom were skeptical about the young Sydney girl. Cut to about five years from then; she found her way to New York when she was offered another job in the Lexington Avenue offices of JWT to salvage another troubled business, this time for Unilever.

It was during this time that she really got to know the city—its parks, museums, the famed delis, restaurants, and bars and really enjoyed submerging herself in the entire experience of being a New Yorker, much of it by foot.

Despite the benefits of her career and her love of working in the city, the work was inside a big bowl of male toxicity, and sadly it was too early for the #metoo movement. While I always think Wild Honey saved me from myself, I think it also saved Stephanie, as it allowed her to give up her punishing role and connect to something that had real meaning for her; it tapped into her innermost talents and passions.

Like me, food plays as the soundtrack to Stephanie's life. In fact, her first career choice was to become a chef, and she even took some steps at Sydney Technical College in Darlinghurst to explore the possibility of doing this. She did not find her passion there at that time and quit after a few short weeks although a love of food and cooking was certifiably in her veins. Stephanie is a superb cook. Her interest in foods, ingredients, the origins and history of great dishes, the stories of chefs, and every new restaurant goes beyond a hobby or passion project. Her ever-expanding library of cookbooks is impressive. It really is part of her existence. Like air and water. And bread.

Conceptualizing the menu for Wild Honey would have been impossible without Steph. And I think it is true that as Wild Honey became more confident, the menus have continued to evolve and find their own footing.

* * *

Stephanie credits much of her love of food and cooking to two people in particular. Her maternal grandmother Bella and her father David. Many of the recipes on our original menu were based on their own recipes—from the scones, waffles and passionfruit sponge cake out of her grandmother's handwritten books to Dad's baked beans, chutneys, and jams out of his own recipe scrapbook.

Bella was, by all accounts, an amazing baker, turning out tray after tray of fresh, piping hot scones every Saturday morning while the exotic coffee beans with a touch of caramel, purchased weekly from the David Jones Food Hall, percolated on the stove. Remember, this was the era of the first wave of coffee, before anyone had heard of Starbucks. Her latticed jam tarts, legendary coffee cake, and passion fruit sponges that were always demanded and made for birthdays; her warm, fluffy steamed puddings turned out with treacle, not to mention her Christmas puddings that would hang in hand-made calico bags in the garage until it was time to light them were legendary.

One of Stephanie's favourite memories is of her grandmother making a sponge cake while she sat atop the bench and watched as the magic of the beater would transform butter and sugar into the palest of pale-yellow mixtures before the eggs were added, and being allowed to lick the beaters once the work was finished. Ironically, baking is one of the things she confesses to not being so good at as she does not have the patience to practise, although I disagree as her pavlova is a veritable work of art, as is her tarte tatin, even in the Singapore humidity.

Steph's father David Senior was also hugely influential in her introduction to gourmet cuisine. He was an avid wine collector and read about food and wine in his spare time. He used to make his own Grand Marnier at home and was an early investor in a camembert company in Mildura, which was sadly ahead of its time and did not succeed. Fun for him was sitting his three children around the table with a napkin to cover the labels of various wines he had chosen and for them to taste and identify them. He had a beautiful wine collection that included Penfolds Grange. He loved to experiment with food and thoroughly enjoyed amassing recipes from magazines and newspapers that he would file into a very messy scrapbook—one that he loved to rifle through to choose something to make for dinner.

He had a knockout recipe for a simple dessert of strawberries and balsamic vinegar and grilled grapefruit for breakfast, and a brilliant seedless green grape with brandy, brown sugar, and sour cream for dessert. But David's forte was really the BBQ that he loved so much. He ferried an old piece of an iron plough-shear in the boot of the car wrapped in newspaper, all ready for any time they might just spontaneously stop for a picnic and BBQ.

It is funny, the first time we had avocado on toast together— this was not a thing in Israel or Europe—Steph told me that her father had been making this when they were very young kids back in Australia, finishing it off with salt and a judicious squeeze of fresh lemon juice, which even she thought was a bit strange at the time.

So, I think Stephanie really inherited her food-love, interest, passion and creativity from him. He was proud to be able to take them out to restaurants-dives and more fine dining. He loved to try new food and indulge in what he called a gastronomic adventure, which for him was the best of life and living. They were down-to-earth Aussies, so none of this was about being seen or ticking boxes. It was really about having an adventure in the kitchen and sharing it all with the family and friends. The house always seemed filled with people and things cooking on stoves and in ovens.

Steph occasionally tells us stories of how special events, birthdays, anniversaries, graduations, Christmas, or Easter were spent—always around food and with family and friends. This included the acknowledgment of the end of every school year with a huge feast at the Marigold Chinese restaurant in Sydney's Chinatown. Today, our family life has emulated this, and pretty much every celebration is honoured. Happily for me, I can make up for all the years my family did not celebrate, although, sometimes, it is a challenge to enjoy it with the same abandon and enthusiasm that Steph has.

As she got older and went off to university, Steph and her sister Jane would cook a lot and loved to throw dinner parties for their boyfriends and friends. These were so popular that she was encouraged by everyone to do something with food, to pay for the cost of eating out on a regular basis—'If it was open, I was there. I read about food and new openings all the time'—and to give her an income while at university, she actually started a small business of cleaning and catering. While the bulk of the work was lugging her vacuum cleaner and cleaning materials from house to house and cleaning them top to tail, she gradually did more and more food related work. She helped throw dinner parties for people, doing prep, setting tables, arranging flowers, and catering—from children's parties to cooking full blown dinners.

Growing up, her friends constantly told her that she should open her own place, and she even envisioned that in her far-off future. For quite a while, she was in the thick of advertising and living the life overseas, but eventually this became old and just a hard, thankless slog, and this idea began to take root. Eventually, when it manifested, it was in a different form and place than she could ever have imagined all those years ago.

Just as my meeting with Stephanie helped me blossom, similarly, I think—or would like to think—that meeting me helped give her a fulfilling outlet for her creativity.

Chapter 8

Alexander David Wächs

Stephanie was even more beautiful when she was pregnant with Alex. It was 2001, post 9/11. New York was a mess, but we were focused on the new life we had coming. Our obstetrician was Dr Saul Srommer from the Upper West Side. He was a funny man, Jewish orthodox, and he instructed Stephanie when the contractions began to drink a small glass of red wine. The 4th of February 2002 was a very long night. We arrived at Mt Lenox Hill Hospital in the evening, and Alex was unfortunately in the dangerous breech position. Dr Saul quickly made the decision to deliver via C-section. When Alex was born the next day, he was jaundiced and had to be placed under the blue lamps. None of this was very unusual, but we were proud, nervous, and inexperienced parents, so every detail took on huge importance.

My parents, who were living in New York around this time, came to the hospital to see their first grandson. They were as excited as you would expect first time grandparents to be. In the end, Alex became their only grandchild. I remember that it was a particularly cold winter's day, and we put Alex in the baby chair and headed home to 51st Street. He cried no end when we got home because his room was too cold, but that was about as much drama as Alex ever gave us. We bonded immediately.

He was a very happy baby, and when I carried him in the baby carrier facing me, he would never fail to look up and smile. I knew Alex was the best thing to have happened to me in my life. Suddenly, my purpose and destiny were clearer. I wanted to be a good husband and a fun dad. Alex's birth made me feel whole for the first time in my life.

We would take Alex for long walks in Central Park, and it was my job to fold and unfold the stroller when we got in and out of taxis. Alex went everywhere with us. Despite being new parents, we were still enjoying Manhattan. Stephanie loved eating in the Italian restaurant in the basement of Barney's, dim sum in Chinatown, and lox bagels in Barney Greengrass on the Upper West. I frequented the Jewish Deli's, attended Broadway shows, and relished the anonymity.

Unfortunately, on the family front, things were not going very well. Tensions were growing over what I felt were small and petty incidents. On Passover when we invited my parents and Daniel for a traditional meal, my father offered to cook, but my mother took our consent as an affront to them. How could we invite them and then have my father cook? Did my parents actually speak to each other, I wondered? So, the day became confrontational and hostile. I had to pop out to shop with my parents when they arrived because, apparently, we did not have all the correct ingredients, and they decided to take this opportunity to disparage Stephanie. When the meal was over and my brother Daniel got up to help with the dishes, the fact that we let him offended my mother no end. How dare we let Professor Daniel Wächs do such a menial job? Stephanie was shocked and, of course, my mother's reaction was directed mainly at Stephanie.

In retrospect, it became clear that my parents, sadly, had not accepted our union. They did not approve of Stephanie, and this was incredibly painful for both of us, but especially for Stephanie. She did not understand their rejection, especially because her family was very open and loving towards me. I do not feel we ever recovered from the mean spiritedness of my parents. Soon after celebrating Alex's first birthday together, we decided to move to Brooklyn. Manhattan felt constricted, and the tension with my parents was starting to make it feel oppressive.

* * *

We relocated to Carroll Gardens, an old Italian neighbourhood. It was the safest place in New York. Here, old families ran the neighbourhood and people did not even have to lock their doors at night. The local shopping was fantastic, and we had everything we needed; there was a bakery, butcher, movie theatre, grocer, and even a little toy shop. Alex had his first haircut in a bright red toy fire engine on Smith Street. He cried so much that we needed to stop. Poor baby Alex. 'It takes a village to raise a child' goes the saying. My mother-in-law Judith arrived from Australia to help us. We needed all the help we could get, and Brooklyn gave us the breathing space we needed to relax and enjoy being parents again.

With its Italian American roots, the neighbourhood showed its heritage in the many traditional cafes and shops on Court and Smith Streets. Hip boutiques (we particularly loved Al Dila), cool bars, and trendy restaurants. The pretty leafy thoroughfares were lined with brownstones fronted by lush gardens. This was home to many young families, and we even tried buying a home there but were outbid. I have very fond memories of this place.

We lived on the ground floor of a small building and in the garden behind us was a fig tree. In the summer, we would spend time with Alex in Carroll Park and he would run through it, happy to be free from the confines of the cold winters. Alex and I began to cycle together. I would strap him onto the back of my bike and ride up to the top of Cobble Hill Park to take in the breathtaking view. I enjoyed Mazzola's, which was decorated with vintage Italian road bikes. This bakery had a famous lard bread made with salami, provolone cheese, prosciutto di parma, and black pepper. It was to die for. To finish off the meal, there were small cookies and amazing coffee.

Alex slipped into our lives seamlessly. We continued to enjoy ourselves and our work, and for me, that restlessness had finally begun to settle. Alex made us both very happy. He was a good friend to us even from that young age, always waiting for us to come home. His first word was 'light', and that was apt as Alex to this day lights up any room he walks into with his cheerful and easy disposition.

It was an idyllic time for us but short-lived. Our destiny, it turned out, was elsewhere.

Chapter 9

Asia Calling

The pace of life in New York is relentless, and with a baby more so. Stephanie and I were working crazy long hours, coordinating who rushed home by 6 p.m. each evening before Alex's helper had to leave. We both began to feel like we needed a change of pace and environment. As luck would have it, Stephanie was offered a senior position in London by her company J.W. Thompson. She accepted the offer, and we both tendered our resignations from our jobs in New York. We were very ready for a new chapter, but it was not to be. A few days later, I was busy at home packing when Stephanie came back after work, crushed. She told me the job in London had been given to someone else. Suddenly, there we were in no man's land, ready to leave for London with no job waiting, and having given up our New York flat and jobs, there was no reason to stay.

What do you do when you are stuck between a rock and a hard place? It was a Friday night in New York City, and so we decided a night on the town was called for. It was November, and mirroring our mood, it was snowing and quite miserable. There was really nothing we could do right then about our predicament, so we headed out to commiserate with each other over some wine. We had wanted a change desperately and had welcomed the new opportunity, but we were now at a real loss, stunned by the turn of events.

Huddled up outside this small Italian restaurant in Greenwich Village smoking (smoking in restaurants had been banned by then), we watched this shadow moving towards us like a slo-mo in an old Hollywood movie. As it came into focus, we realized it was Bob Jeffrey, Stephanie's boss. He came right up to us and asked Stephanie how she was. She replied, 'Bob, actually, pretty shitty.' He raised his eyebrow and asked her what the problem was. JWT was such a large global company, he had no idea what had happened and when she told him, he was surprised. He patted her on the shoulder and told her not to worry and to drop in and see him at the office on Monday morning.

We had a sleepless weekend.

On Monday, Stephanie left for that meeting and did not get back from work till extremely late. I could not reach her by phone the entire day, and when she got home, she sat me down and told me she had been offered a job in Bangkok. Without hesitation, I said, 'Let's do it!' Stephanie was a little more cautious. Neither of us had ever been to Thailand, we had a small child, and there was a lot to consider. From my perspective, I thought, just how bad could it be?

Realistically, we did not have much choice; so, we plunged ahead and traveled there for a look-see. We very much liked what we saw, which was probably helped by the fact that we stayed at the stunning riverside Oriental Hotel. We found a wonderful little nursery preschool school for Alex called The Purple Elephant and an apartment in Soi 33 on Sukhumvit Road. We said 'yes' to the move, and this was the beginning of a new adventure.

* * *

We planned to arrive in Bangkok just after Christmas 2004, stopping in Australia on the way for a brief visit to Stephanie's parents. Our trip was delayed by the terrible Boxing Day tragedy, a day no one in South and Southeast Asia will likely forget. An unimaginably immense and powerful tsunami originating off the Indonesian seashore, the deadliest in recorded history, swept through much of the coast of the region, and Thailand reeled from the tragedy. We were already in Australia and watched with horror and despair the events unfolding there.

The chaos and devastation caused by the tsunami delayed our trip and it meant that we had to stay in Australia for quite a while longer. On the upside, this meant extra time with Steph's parents on the Gold Coast in Queensland. My parents-in-law lived in a renovated old Queenslander house on Mt Tamborine. Located in a temperate rainforest, kookaburras are abundant, and the views over the gold coast are spectacular. These houses are unique to the area and are single detached dwellings made of timber with corrugated iron roofs. They are generally set high off the ground, single-storey, and have a distinctive veranda that mostly extends around the house. This vast structure had been expanded to accommodate us in a guest apartment, and the garden was big enough for Alex to spend hours exploring.

I spent my time swimming, driving down to the beaches, and playing with Alex. Stephanie's parents, David Senior and Dr Hancock made every effort to make us feel welcome and loved. David Senior made Alex a billycart, and he would zoom down the slopes whooping with glee. Our wedding in New York had been a small affair, and this gave us the chance to hold a ceremony with family and special friends. We had a French style wedding with a massive croquembouche cake. Then, we even left Alex with his grandparents and took a long overdue honeymoon in Hunter Valley, enjoying the romantic atmosphere of wine country. The Aussies were relaxed and friendly, and it reminded me of Israel. This holiday was very welcome.

When we finally could travel to Thailand in February, the mood was more sombre, coming so soon after the devastation of the 2004 tsunami. Our initial stay was, of course, at the Mandarin Oriental, our all-time favourite hotel in the world. By the time we left, each and every staff member, including the legendary general manager Kurt Wachtveitl knew us by name. We finally left the hotel when our furniture arrived at our flat in TBI Towers on Sukhumvit Soi 33. This was ideally located close to Steph's JWT office and near Alex's pre-school. It was strange. When we had first visited Bangkok on our recce trip, I was standing by the river, and I experienced this powerful déjà-vu. Growing up, my parents had a picture of the floating market in our home and that image had, I think, lodged itself into my subconscious. I felt a visceral connection with the city and the culture, and I often wonder if this might be where we both retire.

Living in Bangkok was a dream. The name means 'City of Angels', and it is also known as the Venice of the East because of the canals that crisscross the city. Bangkok was noisy, smelly, and full of life. I loved it right from the beginning with its vibrant personality, exotic mix of people, animals, vendors, and colourful tuk-tuks (three-wheeler vehicles). Stephanie went straight to work. She had a personal driver, Khun Od, and we had a wonderful helper, Khun Noi, who took very good care of me and especially Alex, as Steph was traveling extensively to visit her clients all over Southeast Asia.

Steph always had a packed suitcase next to our bed ready to go, and in her first year, she spent a whopping 150 days outside of Thailand. The upside was that when she was home, we would take the opportunity to travel to exotic destinations within Thailand, like the beaches of Koh Samet and Hua Hin, the summer Royal Palace in Ayutthaya, and Khao Yai National Park. We enjoyed going to the weekend markets and buying fresh fruits and flowers, and for our regular groceries, we shopped at the nearby Villa Market. Alex began school, and I would drop him off in the morning and meet my friend Andrew Nathan, who was then the managing director of Starbucks Thailand. His daughter, Amanada, and Alex would play together, and he would become an important contact for me when I moved to Singapore.

The move to Bangkok would also lead to the start of a long and enduring relationship with Hans Mueller, the creative director of JWT, who would become instrumental in the opening of Wild Honey. Hans had a beautiful restaurant called Spring and Summer on Sukhumvit Soi 49. He was from the world of advertising and he was very cool and creative. We saw his lifestyle, and we thought we could definitely get used to Bangkok living. The bustling markets, an exotic cuisine that we were excited to discover, a vibrant street life, and mountains and beach resorts within a stone's throw from the city. I cannot deny that the expat life of having a driver, live-in home help, and a large apartment with stunning ornate Thai furniture was a huge pull for us. Most of all, the gentleness of the Thai people was like a soothing balm to us after the madness of New York.

* * *

The kingdom and its people were beautiful, but after a few months of playing homemaker, I felt the need to get back to work. It was not easy to find a local job as a foreigner in Thailand. My interview at the Four Seasons went like this:

GM: You seem to have some experience working in restaurants.

Me: Yes. I think I could improve some of your restaurants.

GM: And how would you do that?

Me: Good cost control, aggressive seating, a marketing campaign, introducing wine events, good public relations, and a few tricks I learned in New York.

GM: How much did you earn in New York?
Me: That's not important. I will start with any salary.
GM: No, but really, how much?
Me: No, no, forget it, it's not important.

I did not get that job, and that conversation was repeated many times over in many different forms. As an expatriate, I would go from hotel to hotel knocking on doors, introducing myself, and offering to work on a local salary and on local terms. Despite this, I was unsuccessful and, they remained suspicious of me. In Thailand, in the hotel industry, I was considered imported goods, not a sought-after commodity, and it was very frustrating for me. Despite being so accessible to the international community and such a significant tourist destination, the job market in Thailand still remains fairly difficult for foreigners to break into. The assumption is always that we expect a much higher pay, and although this was not the case, I did not seem to be able to convince any prospective employers of this fact.

I finally got my big break when my old boss in New York, Peter Wyss, recommended me to the Raffles Hotel group from Singapore which happened to be expanding into Bangkok in 2005 by taking over management of the old Hilton Hotel property in Nai Lert Park. I was interviewed by Blaise Montendon, the general manager, and soon after, he hired me as the manager in charge of service quality at the hotel. I was to oversee the hotel's five restaurants. This would be my first experience working in Asia, my first time working for a Singaporean company, and my first time working with Thais. I had no idea what I was getting myself into but I was determined to work and was grateful for the opportunity. Stephanie was on a generous package and had offered to be the sole breadwinner but I had too much pride to accept that, and I needed to contribute to the household to feel a sense of self-worth.

The job was much more interesting than I could have expected. I quickly realized that the hotel needed me much more than I ever anticipated as none of the staff spoke English. This was a five-star hotel, a Raffles property; English was imperative. I had to train the Thai staff not only in service skills but also in language and culture. Knowing how to receive Singaporeans, because they made up the bulk of our guests, was hugely important to the success of the hotel. So, in addition to being a restaurant manager, I was also, in effect, the training manager.

I desperately wanted to learn Thai, but the HR department forbade me from speaking the local language so that their staff would be drilled into learning English. Ironically, my spoken and written English was not that great either, so at times, it felt like the blind leading the blind. I was teaching them how to greet and converse with guests, and considering my background, I believe I managed to develop into a good teacher. The Thais are extremely gentle, and it was a far cry from aggressive, impulsive New Yorkers. It took me a while to establish trust with the team, but after about six months, they became more responsive to me as they realized that I wanted them to feel pride, to be professional in their behaviour, and this offered concrete goals of developing a career path for them. This was when the real bonding between the Thai hotel staff and me started to happen.

The job was a challenge on many fronts. For me, learning the local culture was fascinating. There were many symbols in their communication, different smiles, little nuances, and it was important that I could read their body language. Thais had an entire language that had nothing to do with linguistics! Then, there was the hotel work. We had to make the guests feel comfortable when they were in the coffee shop, irrespective of the time of the day it was—breakfast, lunch or dinner. It was not a small area either, it extended from the indoor area into a vast outdoor patio overlooking the swimming pool and the park. I managed all this while I darted around in my three-piece suit in that sticky and humid climate. I sweated profusely.

It also definitely challenged me at many other levels. I needed to learn more about Asian and Thai food as the menu was quite international. The Thai royal family, the then Prime Minister Thaksin, and one of the first owners of Raffles and the Minister of Transportation frequented the hotel. So, I was being exposed to important lessons in how to interact with the elite of Thailand, who were, of course, very different to the New York elite! This was high society at another level. The Minister of Transportation was the first woman minister, Khun Sampatisiri, and her father was a business tycoon having made his fortune in, of all things, ice making. She had taken over the ice factories from her father and knew nothing about running hotels but wanted in on this prestigious project. There was this odd triangle of high society investors, the old Hilton Hotel infrastructure (who had managed the property initially), and now the Singapore Raffles Group, my employers.

It is interesting when I look back at my first introduction to Thai culture. It was actually at a kitchen in New York City. When I was working for Restaurant Associates in New York, we had an all-Thai team in the kitchen. One of the cooks decided to play a joke on me one evening, and he made me pad thai, a traditional Thai noodle dish. A mainstay of any Thai restaurant's menu, pad thai is flat rice noodles fried with prawns, tofu, and egg with a sour tamarind and salty fish sauce base. It is generously sprinkled with spring onions, roasted peanuts, and sugar to offset the topping of dry red chilli powder. When I was served the pad thai by the cook, he covered the noodles with a very generous amount of those dry red chili flakes.

Being the dope that I am, I ate the whole thing without realizing the strength of the chilli, and I became very, very sick. Thai chilli is ten, maybe even one hundred times stronger than

anything I had tasted before. I found out later that it was an
allergic reaction. Nevertheless, at that moment, I did not know
how to handle my dissatisfaction with this individual who
played this trick on me. I admit it was funny, but I was also very
ill as a result. I did not want to use my power as a manager to
punish him, but when he needed something from me later, I
resisted and he became a little bit aggressive, and I became more
aggressive, and I finally told him off for the prank. For him, it
was nothing, and he had forgotten about it.

When I moved to Thailand, the abundance of chilli in
that cuisine made me realize that he might have put the chilli
there as flavour! For the Thais, that amount of chilli was really
nothing. In fact, when the Thai team in New York heard that
I was moving to Bangkok, they made a list of their relatives'
phone numbers and gave it to me. 'You call, you call,' they told
me earnestly, anticipating that I might need help in a new city.
I arrived in Bangkok with that list of names of drivers, nurses,
babysitters, and even soldiers and generals. I never called any of
them, but I carried that list around with me for ages, and it gave
me a great sense of reassurance that someone was looking out
for me. Thinking of their generosity still puts a smile on my face,

This was a beautiful country with equally charming people.
The food and culture were all new to us. Remember that this was
a Jewish man, who had grown up in Israel and Europe, and an
Australian woman from Sydney, both moving to Thailand from
New York. Being in the kitchen was exhilarating, an overload
of new colours, smells, and tastes. Thai cuisine mixes sweet and
salty, fruit and main courses, and garnishing can often be the star
of the show. It was an introduction to a new world of cooking.
In the meantime, we enjoyed the warmth of the Thais. This was
our period of travel, adventure, and risk-taking. We tried new
things in a society that could not have been more different from
the United States. In the US, it was all about the individual, and

in Thailand, suddenly we were thrust into this society that was all inclusive. It was a culture shock of the very best kind.

Alex's time at the Purple Elephant Montessori was phenomenal, and the fact that we got a dog meant that we were really settled there. We ate on the streets and chatted with vendors; it was a simpler life than what I was used to in New York, and, of course, the warm weather helped. Working in Thailand as a foreigner was very challenging, but from a cultural perspective, it was incredible. In a way, it prepared me for that all important step to Singapore. Ironically, Thailand was great to live in, but it was difficult to work there. Singapore would be the opposite, fantastic to work in but it took us much longer to find the joys of living there.

The Singapore Raffles brand speaks to tradition, quality, and breeding. It is the royal brand of Singapore. This was an amazing way to be introduced to Singapore and Singaporeans. The Singaporean guests who came to the Raffles in Bangkok were very well travelled; they had high standards and expectations. They were people with the means to make these demands. It was a real eye-opener for me. I think the Western assumption is that Asians do not know Western food, but nothing could be further from this belief. The Singaporeans I met had travelled to Australia and Europe; they understood Western cuisine very well. They had refined tastes, and you could not afford to underdeliver or outsmart them, or it would come back to knock you like a boomerang. It was a sharp learning curve for me. I remember that if we put five types of cheese on the buffet, the Singaporeans would ask why there were not eight choices. If we put out eight types of cheese, Singaporeans would be expecting sixteen varieties. In other words, good was never enough and that early experience prepared me for the Singaporean market. You have to constantly improve as the target is always moving, and Singaporeans, being straight to the point, will help guide you there.

Family life in Thailand continued to be enriched by our frequent holidays. We particularly enjoyed Loi Krathong, the celebration of the goddess of water, where people release intricate handmade lotus-shaped rafts decorated with candles and incense onto the water, gleefully spraying each other with water, and generally partying on the streets. One year, we drove for two days from the capital to the north of Thailand (Chiang Mai) and visited Sukhothai, the old capital. I was altogether impressed with the taste and creativity of the local culture. I bought an old Vespa scooter and would zoom around Thong-Lor Street with Alex on the back. We got a small black and white dog called Truly, and Alex and I would train and walk her together. She came with us on the move to Singapore and lived till she was fifteen years old.

We became members at the British Club and enjoyed playing tennis, swimming, and going to the gym. Alex celebrated his fourth birthday with ponies and lots of friends. During our introduction to the British Club, we met Eilat Shoshana and her children. She was from Israel, and we became good friends. She was always cooking up a storm and opened her home for everyone to enjoy. I especially enjoyed spending the Jewish holidays at their home, and, sometimes, they would go on long road trips to exotic islands, and Alex and I would join their adventures exploring Thailand. The nature and wildlife was spectacular. I remember hoping that tourism would not destroy those habitats, and, in a strange twist, Covid-19 has helped preserve our fragile planet. The chaos and traffic in Bangkok reminded me of the *balagan* or as we say in Hebrew, the mess, in Israel. We enjoyed living there so much.

Little did we know that our time in Bangkok would come to an end sooner than expected.

* * *

In 2006, after a military coup in Thailand, foreign businesses grew increasingly uncomfortable as the tax situation became less favourable, and Stephanie's client Unilever decided to move their regional headquarters to Singapore. This meant Stephanie, as their global business director, would be relocated. That meant we all would move. By this time, we were feeling comfortable with Asia and a move to Singapore did not feel like the worst thing. In fact, in some ways, for a young family, it felt like an upgrade.

So, in 2008, we suddenly found ourselves in Singapore. We enrolled Alex, who was now four years old, at United World College of South East Asia, an international school, and Stephanie went straight to work. Déjà-vu. I needed to reinvent myself yet again. This time, it was easier. I got a job through a connection in Bangkok, and I was hired to open the first Wine Connection restaurant in Singapore at Robertson Walk. Unfortunately, that did not last long; the owner and I had professional differences over the future direction of that business, and I left.

This is when the move to Singapore really hit me. I did not have a job, was a stay-at-home dad and had no idea what my future was. How was I going to find a job that would really make me happy? The thought of yet another job hunt and delivering to yet another boss did not appeal to me. I looked around and realized that I had gotten very used to Thailand. Singapore was squeaky clean, a futuristic city, a computer-generated version of a real city like you might see on the television series *Westworld*. I asked myself what I was doing there. I missed the vibrant, pungent, noisy streets of Bangkok with the zipping tuk-tuks and the soft welcoming smiles. I could not find my bearings at all, and, at one point, I said to Stephanie, 'Hey let's move back to Bangkok.' But moving back was not going to happen, so I had to find myself, my mojo, an existence that would make me feel comfortable living here. I realized that I would not find

it by frequenting Orchard Road or Marina Bay Sands, or on
Sentosa. I had to find it through things that were important to
me. I needed to go back to work, but I felt stuck.

It was Stephanie who knew what I needed better than I
did. She could see my restlessness and finally tapped me on
the shoulder and said, 'Hey, why don't you just open your own
business? Open your own restaurant.' I remember giving her
the most incredulous stare, and I said, 'Why the "F" would I
do that to myself? After everything that happened to my dad.
After everything that I've experienced in my industry over the
last twenty years. Why would I subject myself to such a horrible
life?' Stephanie with her wisdom and vision said, 'Because if
you're willing to do it for hotels, and you're willing to do it for
other owners, why not do it for yourself?'

What an eye opener for me. She was right. I had sacrificed
a lot working for other people, working on weekends and public
holidays, and I had never questioned why I was doing it. Yes, to
earn money, but I never stopped to ask myself where this was
heading in terms of my own career goals. I had never stopped to
think about trying to do it for myself. I had the answer, and the
reason for this was simple: it was too risky! Having worked for
over twenty years in the hospitality industry, I knew that opening
a restaurant could be financial suicide and would require 24/7
total dedication. I had watched the burnout in this industry,
the alcoholism, the broken marriages, and besides, what I had
been through, watching my father struggle, had taught me a
lesson that had been absorbed into my psyche: never ever open
a restaurant unless you want to burn through your money and
then fail.

On the flip side, I had been keenly observing the restaurant
scene in Singapore as a customer. Eating out in Singapore was
a profound disappointment to me. Singapore was the Mecca
of food in so many ways, an amalgamation of Malay, Indian,

and Chinese cuisines, but not for Western dining. The Western dining scene was based on American chains and coffee, bread, and fresh produce was basic. Granted, Jones the Grocer, the cafe imported from Sydney, had just opened their flagship restaurant and deli in the lifestyle destination of Dempsey Hill. It was impressive with a cheese cave, flower shop, massive kitchen with high ceilings, and the retail food section reminded me of Harrods food market in London. However, despite Jones, there were still massive gaps in the market. As a couple with a young son, we struggled to find quality restaurants to dine out at, especially for weekend brunches, an important family time. Hotel buffets with their gluttonous spreads and equally inflated cost were not suited to provide a casual but quality breakfast in a welcoming relaxed environment where our son could frolic freely. Would not it be nice if, like in Sydney, we had a place we liked going to for brunch where Alex would be welcome? Would not it be nice if we could have breakfast after 11 a.m.?

Would not it be nice if we could have eggs for dinner?

Chapter 10

Nuts and Bolts

I do love breakfast; it is my favourite meal of the day. Israeli breakfasts are famous for being healthy and light with no meat, just a lot of yogurts, veggies, eggs, and of course our very own pita bread! When I travelled to Australia in 2004, I was blown away by the creativity and the coffee culture. The Aussies do the best brunch, no joke. Enjoying breakfast and desiring a place to go was a far cry from opening your own restaurant, but the thought of doing something new and exciting was growing on me.

In a matter of weeks, I decided to take a breather and think about these new ideas. Tel Aviv is where ideas come together for me; moreover, I had my old friend Boaz Dolgin the *fein schmecker* (German for food connoisseur) there. We went to a place called Benedict on Ben Yehuda Street. Lo and behold, they served breakfast 24/7. I loved the concept. It was fun, young, and sexy. What makes you happier than the smell of fresh bread, homemade jam, cinnamon, coffee beans, and strawberries? It was a symphony for the nose. I thought, how playful, how nice to do something around breakfast. I came back to Singapore, and I said, 'Hey, I found this amazing concept in Israel. Stephanie, why don't we open an all-day breakfast restaurant? Why don't we open the *first* all-day breakfast restaurant in Singapore?'

I was starting to feel that sense of purpose again, a tingle of excitement, a prickling of possibility. Then Stephanie was at a business meeting in New York in a boardroom with our old friend from Bangkok, Hans Muller, and was mulling over names for the restaurant when she suddenly jotted down 'Wild Honey'. Hans loved it because he said that like honey, it sticks. I was ambivalent about this name, but Stephanie knew a winner when she saw one. I would realize later that the initials of Wild Honey, WH, were the initials of our last names, Wächs and Hancock. Stephanie, of course, already knew that.

So, now we had an idea—all-day breakfast—and a name— Wild Honey. After that, where do you start to open a business?

* * *

First, you find the capital. Stephanie invested US $400,000, which had to cover Research & Development, agents, deposits, designers, fitting out, permits, equipment, and much, much more. Luckily, one of the strengths I had developed in my career was cost control. The other advantage I had was that I was absolutely terrified to lose money because of a mistake. I created Wild Honey Private Limited, and opened a business account. Stephanie asked Hans to help with a logo and Hans added the tagline 'Wild Honey—No Place Like Home'. What genius! Hans had put our entire ethos into four words. I remember seeing the logo for the first time; Stephanie and I were over the moon.

No Place Like Home

A key factor for F&B retail is its location. The hundred-thousand-dollar question was: where? I was cruising locations on my newly purchased Vespa and getting more familiar with the neighbourhoods. The places I explored included Holland Village, bohemian and bustling, a combination of 80s charm, with new upmarket outlets and old mom and pop shops. The tried and tested location of Dempsey, an expansive hilly green area with antique shops and creative new eateries brimming with potential. Then there was Turf City, scheduled to go through a massive overhaul in 2009 to turn this horse racing hub into a vision the developers had not quite conceptualized yet. It was very rundown and the demographic was wrong for us. Another location was right around the corner from our condo in Jaya Tower at Evans Road, a tiny enclave on the edge of the iconic Botanic gardens, the popular running track and next to a small student hostel. It was not quite right for us

I turned to my friend Andrew Nathan from Thailand. Parents of children in the same school your child attends can prove to be invaluable contacts, and as the managing director of Starbucks, he had a lot of contacts. Andrew introduced us to Steven Goh, who himself had been with Starbucks Singapore and was then the Director of the Orchard Road Business Association (ORBA). So, this introduction made sense as all of us were in the same business. This meeting and subsequent friendship became pivotal to our success in Singapore. Steven's warmth and willingness to guide us consistently through the process of opening Wild Honey showed a generosity of spirit that we slowly learned also existed in Singapore.

Steven agreed to meet me for coffee near his office in Tanglin Shopping Center. It rained heavily that day, and I turned up at the coffee shop soaked to the skin. I must have presented myself as an odd fellow, arriving on my Vespa dripping wet. Steven asked good questions and was extremely knowledgeable about the F&B retail scene on Orchard Road. He introduced me to the calculation of rental space into seats (covers), and this would help us project our future profits. I left this meeting supercharged and more motivated than ever before. Steven became my mentor in Singapore and our subsequent friendship became pivotal to our success

Through Steven, we were introduced to Adeline Tan, a property agent from CBRE real estate company. My calculations said our ideal restaurant would be small, about 1,500 square feet. This would have to include the 50 seats which I used for my projections. Stephanie suggested searching on Orchard Road. This was the big league. Singapore's High Street. Retail Central. Were we ready for such a grand beginning?

Mandarin Gallery sits almost smack in the middle of Orchard Road, below the Mandarin Meritus Orchard hotel, which is one of the few 1,000-room hotels in Singapore. It was going through a two-year renovation. The idea of opening Wild Honey in a hotel gallery made total sense as, right from the beginning, we thought a 24/7 breakfast place would be popular with hotel patrons. The fact that the gallery was attached to one of the island's biggest hotel properties fit in with our plans perfectly. The mall was set to open in December 2009; that gave us a timeline of nine months. We presented our idea to Patrina Tan, GM of Overseas Union Enterprise, the managers of the Gallery, and she shared her vision of the future tenant mix of both retail and F&B.

We decided from the outset that Wild Honey would become a fashion centric brand. We chose Orchard Road as our location because it is the High Street of Singapore, similar to 5th Avenue in New York or the Champs-Élysées in Paris. Level 3 of the Gallery was to have only retail shops, but Stephanie requested that unit 03–02 be converted to an F&B space because she already had a vision that Wild Honey and retail would go hand in hand, getting us high visibility by associating our brand with retail rather than other restaurants. Indeed, we were right! We were frequented by fashion photographers, actors, singers, models and industry captains, and once a year during fashion week, Orchard Road turns into a massive catwalk, and Wild Honey becomes a hotbed of beautiful people! Unit 03–02 was only 1,256 square feet, smaller than we hoped, but it was overlooking Orchard Road and had natural daylight. Stephanie and I like to look at food in natural light, and we felt that daylight was important to the ambiance of an all-day breakfast concept. It was soft, bright, and cheery, and you could even see some greenery from the trees outside on Orchard Road.

* * *

We had a name and location and then things became much more serious. We had nine months to find a designer, apply for permits, find a chef, create a menu, find suppliers, and deal with all the unexpected details that would come our way. The interior of Wild Honey would be critical for our branding and for enticing customers. We needed to find the right designer, and this was a huge challenge. In Singapore, the big firms were not interested in a small project like Wild Honey, so we once again fell back on our friend Hans Müller in Bangkok. He introduced us to a designer-turned-teacher Khun Q, who was more experienced in home design and less in commercial design. It was perfect for our no-place-like-home concept. When I made a Skype call to Khun Q, he suggested that I work with his students but I was uncomfortable. How much experience do students have in real life? Plus, I operate on instinct, and I felt Khun Q was the right person to design the interiors of Wild Honey. I tried my very best to convince him that this project was worthy and would win awards in the future (I was not being truthful). My tenacity and persistence, my Jewish *chutzpah*, and perhaps my little deception paid off. However, the deal was that I would be project manager and he would manage it remotely.

Then, it was time to find an architect and main contractor for our project. Luckily for us, business was down, so everyone was looking for work. I turned to Steven Goh. He recommended we meet with Steven Lew, owner of Quan Mei Design as they had worked together on some F&B retail projects. We met at PS Cafe in Dempsey and fortunately Khun Q was visiting Singapore for a conference, so he was able to join this critical meeting. From the moment I met Steven Lew, I was calm and relaxed. He was honest and very positive about our fledgling project and totally understood Khun Q's vision. We shook hands and conducted a site inspection in Mandarin Gallery. The space was totally open with no walls and completely empty, and yet felt welcoming and comfortable. I started to imagine our new kitchen, bar, dining room, entrance, and it became a fairy-tale in the making.

It was time for Stephanie to get more involved. Stephanie had a very clear and artistic point of view on how Wild Honey would feel. She has a magical talent of matching things and highlighting certain details that I do not notice, and she started to work with us on the mood and material board. Khun Q had brought some materials from Bangkok, and we began to get a picture of the design. Khun Q liked French Blue as the colour, and brass, wood, and all natural fabrics and materials for the rest of the concept. Stephanie has terrific taste in decoration, and she added a level of sophistication and a feminine touch that I could never bring to the table. The space would feel like French kitchen meets a loft in New York City. It was going to be Tel Aviv in Singapore. I was so excited. I loved it.

We went to Bangkok to source materials and at the same time revisited our old haunts. Spring & Summer on Soi 49 Sukhumvit, Kuppa on Soi 11, GreyHound Cafe, and the Jim Thompson Museum. We re-enjoyed the markets: weekend markets, flower markets, and night markets. Seeing all these markets also gave me something to worry about. All this fresh food would not be so easy in Singapore. The majority of fresh food in Singapore is imported from Australia, Malaysia, Thailand, Japan, USA, and Europe. I kept a mental note that this would be something I would have to deal with later. While shopping for Wild Honey, I wandered into a thrift shop on Soi Thung and was smitten with an old Bang & Olufsen radio. I thought it would look so perfect in the restaurant, but I did not buy it. When Khun Q arrived in Singapore the day before we opened, he had that B&O radio with him. Stephanie had arranged for its purchase and it still sits in Wild Honey as a centrepiece. Bangkok is like that, a treasure trove of unexpected finds. I was touched by Stephanie's gesture.

We returned to Singapore full of new ideas and were excited about the furniture design. Khun Q had started drawing the furniture, and the plan was to produce them in Bangkok and ship them to Singapore. Other material was sourced locally by Steven Lew. We were on a budget, so some choices reflected that. For instance, the gold spotlights were bought from that good, old staple, Ikea. The artwork would be created by a good friend of Stephanie, Deirdre Strang, a painter from Sydney. There would be an espresso bar that would allow people to stand and drink coffee like in Italy. Fresh flowers, bread, and cake on the retail display were all part of the elements that helped create the magic. The name and the fact that honey was an important part of the menu inspired one crazy idea to use a real honeycomb as a decorative piece. I decided to drive up to Malacca on the coast of West Malaysia to a bee farm and buy royal honey. While there, I could not resist buying the honeycomb. It was carefully inserted into a protective glass jar and displayed in the retail cabinet alongside the flowers, breads, and jams. One day, a few years later, to my horror, I noticed maggots living inside the honeycomb and it was quickly discarded!

The menus were handwritten on black boards displayed behind the bar and cashier area. The shopfront would have large doors with copper handlebars and the base would be wood. Khun Q's vision was a playful inside-outside concept to arouse the curiosity of passers-by. Another unique feature was Stephanie's idea of using old wooden floorboards. Steven was able to source old railroad tracks from Malaysia. They would be treated to look very old. Red bricks occupy a small wall in the back, test tubes with flowers decorate the wall, and a magazine rack features music, design, and art magazines for our guests. All these details were to make Wild Honey feel more like a grandmother's living room rather than a restaurant. A signature of our design was the decision that the tables and chairs would not match, and each one would be different. Mismatching would make it more interesting and give each table its own DNA. A Gucci Prada table 1, a love sofa for the couples, table 8 for staff interviews and people who like to read. It was a wonderland in a tiny space; thought and effort went into every aspect of the design, and we loved it, and, as it turned out, so would our guests.

* * *

The next question was, who was going to design the all-important kitchen? I remembered, when going to a submarine museum with Alex on one of our trips to Australia, I was fascinated by how small the kitchen was. That memory came back because my calculations of 30 per cent kitchen space meant that the kitchen was going to be very, very tight. Luxuries like a walk-in chiller, a pantry, a pastry kitchen; they were just not realistic. I needed a kitchen expert who could help make sure that every square inch would be utilized. When I was working as a young restaurant manager in Bangkok at the Swissotel, Andreas Nasuer was the executive chef. He had also worked in Davos, and I had met him there when I would go skiing with my grandmother, Edith. He was talented and had won the Best French Restaurant and Best Wine List awards in Bangkok for Ma Maison in 2005. Andreas was now in Singapore working as a chef culinary instructor at the SunRice institute in Fort Canning. I asked for his help. We met for a beer and a smoke and brainstormed on how to make this kitchen work. I even offered him the position of head chef at Wild Honey, but he politely declined.

The kitchen design resulted in an L-shape, which meant dishes out in the front for food service, and dishes in from the back for stewarding. One obvious defect of this design was that the supplies had to come in the front, the prep area was small, and storage tight. With this kitchen, the future menu would only be able to offer a limited choice of dishes and so innovation became critical at this point. Andreas wanted everything to be parallel, for instance, the fridges and the cooking range, to ensure that the cooks did not need to move anything from left to right. We practised standing together tied with strings to see how the cooks would work side-by-side. This technique was used in French kitchens to improve flow and communication because it forces individuals to work in unison and harmony by synchronizing their movements. Everything about this relationship worked perfectly. Andreas was highly methodical, which I could relate to, and like the success of the strings process, I knew that this kitchen would prove to be an invaluable asset.

Now, it was time to find a head chef and work on the menu.

Chapter 11

Ready, Steady, Go

How do you search for a head chef in Singapore? There were over ten thousand restaurants in the city, but why would any chef work for Wild Honey? It was risky and unproven. I decided to advertise in the *Straits Times's* 'Help Wanted' section: 'Singaporean Chef with Aussie experience'.

My first interview was with Jimmy Mun. We met at the Starbucks in Paragon and that first meeting lasted three hours. Jimmy was my only choice, my first choice, and the right choice. Jimmy had graduated from the Shatec Culinary School, did his practical training at the W hotel, and had worked in Queensland Australia for a year. Jimmy was very talented with R&D, and I liked his scientific approach to cooking. As always, working on instinct (this has always proved to be so important in my business), I offered him the job. The very next day, Jimmy received an offer from another restaurant, but he chose Wild Honey, and the rest, as they say, is history.

We needed to conceptualize and create a menu. Since we did not have a place to work and test our ideas, Stephanie decided we would use our condo in Jaya Tower. We purchased all the materials at the Cold Storage supermarket on Bukit Timah Road. This was R&D on the fly, no commercial kitchen or big investors, just our humble kitchen in our condominium, which was nearly destroyed in the process! The core idea was a global breakfast menu. My sister-in-law Jane had sent me a similar all-day-breakfast menu from The European Cafe in Brisbane and another inspiration was Benedict in Tel Aviv. Jimmy and I would work on the menu while taking culinary direction from Stephanie and Andreas.

The first draft had sixteen breakfast items including Tunisian, European, Canadian, and what we called Sweet Morning. We would invite Singaporean friends, like my neighbour Conny Lew, for tasting sessions. A panel would grade us on things like flavour, value, presentation, and portioning. Another advisor was Alan Wong, a wine importer for Ruffino Wines in SE Asia whose family owned the Shangri-La Hotel company. Alan suggested a positioning of over $18.00 for each main dish. He believed that if we over delivered on portion size and flavour, then people would pay those prices. 'The more the better,' he said. The high price point would set us apart from all the other breakfast type restaurants yet be affordable compared to hotels. We needed to hit the sweet spot.

The genius of it was that we actually ended up creating a new category for all-day breakfast. On one side, there was the utilitarian Starbucks and other coffee chains and on the other the overindulgent Champagne Brunch at the Line in Shangri-La. What we created was the middle category, affordable luxury as Stephanie described it. The formula was perfect. The high ticket allowed us to use premium imported ingredients and cook international food but for the Singaporean palate. This was critical. We wanted Wild Honey to be loved by Singaporeans. Why? Respect and practicality; there are more Singaporeans, and in a recession, like in 2008, (and a pandemic like 2020), they do not move away. In addition, there was a certain point of pride in attracting customers from the exacting local market.

Fast forward to 2021. Imagine if we had not built this local base, what would have happened to us?

Research became critical. Jimmy would go to the local markets on the West Coast to survey fresh produce. He was an Apple (no not the fruit) freak and insisted on only using Mac devices. He introduced me to a software called ShopNCook that computed the cost of goods, wrote recipes, and measured nutritional information based on USDA standards. This tool allowed us to calculate our food cost for future dishes.

Throughout this process, administrative matters had to be dealt with. I needed a certified public accountant. I found Seewai through a flyer and hired him part time, meeting once a week for an hour. Budgeting was crucial and outsourcing became my strategy in many areas including uniform rentals, dishwashing machines, ovens, coffee machines, CCTV, stewarding, and human resources for recruitment. In some cases, I was even lucky enough to get equipment sponsored, which helped me save $50,000. I knew Frederick from Victoria Coffee Australia and I asked him to sponsor a coffee machine. Jimmy contacted an old school friend Eileen from SynTech Chemicals, and she sponsored our dishwasher. We still use SynTech Chemicals today. Andreas used his Swiss connection with the owner of Swissbake, Xavier Baume, who sponsored a combo oven. These relationships lasted for many years and were very meaningful for us. We decided to use flatware crockery on white, in a classic French style, and purchased kitchen equipment from Sia Huat on Temple Street. For heavy kitchen equipment, we worked with a company that specialized in fast food chains. This was all taking place at breakneck speed to meet our opening day deadline, and, in the midst of all this, the menu had to be created.

* * *

A recipe card in the kitchen is what chords are to a jazz musician; without the basics, the methodology, you cannot create anything. They are about how to prepare the food, but they will not help you create the magic. Imagine a yoga studio trying to maintain the intellectual property of its practices? It would never work. In the same way, cooking is universal. Recipes are shared across so many platforms, and we used them all! Books like *Bill's* by Bill Granger from Australia, Sabta Edith's Czech cheese dumplings and her Bircher muesli recipe, and contributions from David senior and Stephanie's mother and grandmother. I loved a moist and fluffy sponge cake and Judith gifted us this recipe and our first jam-making pot. My father Gabriel arrived from Miami and helped Jimmy with basic pastry and our first lemon tart. One day, my son Alex had a playdate with a Brazilian boy from school and when his grandma came to collect him and noticed me in the kitchen, she kindly suggested teaching us a Brazilian dish called Pancho Kase, which we named Brazil Balls. It was delicious and to this day it is a Wild Honey bestseller. Like music, the chords are just the steppingstone to that chart topping hit, so the recipe cards had to be fine-tuned to create our bestsellers.

The menu of course focused on eggs. Poached, scrambled, sunny side, omelettes, baked. The bread would be delivered to us half-baked so we could do the final bake on site. This would ensure freshness. The idea of duplicating ingredients wherever possible ensured less wastage and more output. All the sauces, basic stocks, pastry, batters, and jams would be made fresh inhouse. We wanted each dish to stick out and remind our customers of something: a trip overseas, a childhood outing, or just a comfortable place. I am a big believer in the importance of consistency in food. Sometimes, Stephanie and I would have a good meal and decide to go back again, but on the second visit, we would be deeply disappointed by the food. We noticed this to be more so in Singapore than other cities. This was a mistake I was determined Wild Honey would never make.

We needed to overdeliver on the portion with a sense of generosity, and the plating would be simple but show finesse. In those days, it was impossible to get edible flowers or micro greens, so the garnishing was simpler, and we used chives, chervil, Italian parsley, icing sugar, and chili powder. The way we cooked our eggs became paramount. Perfection on a plate. We would sell tea breads in coconut and banana, beautiful cupcakes in blueberry, chocolate, and strawberry flavours, buttermilk pancakes, and Belgian waffles. We made our own yoghurts and hung some of them to create white cheese, known as labneh in Arabic. Batters were made fresh every day and had the texture of silk when you ate them. The kids went crazy for our sweets and they are some of the biggest fans of Wild Honey.

Beverages needed to be curated, so I turned to the Swedish Bar Mafia created by Benny Ben David. That of course was my nickname for these talented youngsters. I needed help with a fresh and customized beverage programme that would complement the food offerings. I knew Benny Sorum from when we had worked together at the Swissotel in Nai Lert Park in Bangkok. He was chief mixologist at the hotel's SYN bar. His team consisted of Danny, Thomas and Ben. Since leaving the hotel, Benny had created a highly successful consulting company called FLOW. These three young men were flying mixologists who would attend events to curate drinks and even catered at the World Economic Forum in Davos where they met people like Bill Gates and Bono from U2. They would also open the Rocket Bar concept in Bangkok some years later and sell it for a nice chunk of change and cater to the VIPs at the F1 events in Singapore.

I invited Benny and his crew to Singapore and the three deadly-handsome Swedish boys arrived with their 007 suitcase fully loaded with the paraphernalia needed to create something unique for Wild Honey. I loved their approach to mixology as it mirrored our cooking. Everything was made from scratch, flavours were pure and concentrated, and they never used pre-mixes. Elements such as flavour, freshness, presentation, balance, and the finish were all considered. The result was a short list of bestsellers: Queen Bee, Nature's Remedy, Miss Bee, Manuka Shakreto, and Mandarin Wilderness.

While we were preparing, the F&B scene in Singapore was evolving. In 2009, 40 Hands by the world champion barista Harry Grover from Perth launched, and his cafe changed the coffee culture in Singapore. It also put the Tiong Bahru neighbourhood on the map. Local residents complained that his cafe was too popular and parking was impossible for them. What they forgot to mention was that their property value had gone up, so thank you Harry for that. This was actually good news because the more sophisticated coffee culture became in Singapore, the better for us.

Finally, we were ready to go, what I called 'all conditions green'. We broke ground with Stephanie and I wearing our Sunday best and hard hats, and we opened a bottle of Champagne. We used spray paint on the floor to mark the kitchen, the bar, the retail area, and furniture sizes. Materials began to arrive, and I would visit the site each day, take pictures and report back to Khun Q in Bangkok. His attention to detail was astonishing, and he had X-ray vision; every minute I worked with him confirmed that my choice of designer had been right.

* * *

There were hiccups; this was to be expected. It was only when we installed the exhaust hood that we realized it was too low, and if the line cooks were not careful, they would bang their heads while cooking. We just had to live with it. Another surprise was when the gas company dropped the gas meter in the wrong location outside the kitchen. I nearly had a heart attack. This had to be relocated as there was no living with this one.

I now started to zoom in on the operations. I knew staffing was going to be a major challenge, and I would need to minimize that component and make this outlet as efficient as possible while still keeping a high level of hospitality. Since the menu was posted on the black boards, I decided to take a Starbucks approach and insisted that guests place orders with the cashier, which would be me. This would allow me to chat with them and recommend and up-sell items. It also meant that once the transaction was settled, the bar and kitchen could start the order instantly, helping with speed and turnover. It proved to be very successful, if not always popular.

Uniforms were designed by Stephanie and Khun Q and produced in Bangkok. The idea was a butcher's apron in utilitarian brown with the Wild Honey logo printed in a rich gold. It was innovative and fun while useful large pockets and heavy buckles gave it an industrial feel. We introduced iPad with images of the fare on the counters. Music would come from the radio, of which I am a big fan. The station was to be KCRW from Santa Monica, California, spinning global beats on Eclectic 24.

Many unexpected expenses surprised me such as deposits, insurance for public liability and cash in transit, cash on delivery for goods and supplies, import tax, and transportation from Singapore Port for the furniture shipped from Bangkok. What a nightmare! I was bleeding money and we had not even opened yet. How did other people do this? I just needed to keep faith and trust my training and experience to survive this test.

* * *

A key thing happened just before opening. Since the mall was not occupied with tenants yet, the owners asked Wild Honey to host a breakfast for the press the day before our opening. Can you imagine the extra stress? We showcased our drinks, served Japanese breakfast bento boxes with round Tamago omelette balls, wasabi mayo and rice; Sri Lankan pancakes; stuffed French toast with grilled Thai mango; vanilla mascarpone aka Sweet Morning, and fresh bread baskets with homemade jams. It turned out to be a huge bonus for us because the press ate it up, quite literally. The food was completely finished! In the *Straits Times* 'Life' section on 26 November 2009, Eunice Quek wrote an article titled 'Mandarin Mall Reopens'. She quoted a Mr Guy Wächs, 30, director of Wild Honey. They made me ten years younger than I was. Of course, I never complained. The quote ran: 'We have looked at the food scene in Singapore and feel that having an all-day-breakfast concept can be a little crazy, but for a strategic location such as Mandarin Gallery, it's a good idea and a good partnership.'

That night, Steph, Andreas, and little Alex—who was only seven years old—were mopping the floors frantically and having animated discussions trying to imagine what would happen on opening day. Would people come? After all, the restaurant was located on Level 3 of a shopping mall. Who would come? What would they order?

At 9.00 a.m. on Friday, 27 November 2009, nine months and four days after Stephanie tapped my shoulder and said 'Hey, why don't you open your own restaurant', Wild Honey opened.

Chapter 12

It's Breakfast—Spread the Word

Just telling my story up to this point has exhausted me. I was running on empty by the time Wild Honey opened and, like a roller coaster after a wild up and down pauses at the top before the next wild lurch, I would like to pause. There are so many things I want to share about Wild Honey. So, before I continue any further with my story, come with me as I take you through some of the key considerations, key moments, and key ideas that contributed to the success of Wild Honey and just how far it has come since opening day.

* * *

Breakfast

Breakfast is like the stepchild, the orphan of the gastronomic world. In Singapore in 2009, there were no all-day breakfast restaurants. Since Wild Honey opened, all-day breakfast has slowly become part of the culture in Singapore. Why would it not? Eggs are consumed voraciously by Singaporeans. All over Singapore, in housing estate coffee shops, boiling water is poured over two eggs in a small plastic mug and a metal cover is placed on top. A plastic basket holds a pepper shaker and soya sauce for garnish. The cover is removed after three to five minutes, depending on if the eggs are supposed to be runny or slightly firmer. This, along with two pieces of toast and coffee, was (and still is) one of the staple Singaporean breakfast dishes in hawker centres all over the island. However, when it came to higher end restaurants, chefs usually looked down on breakfast as a non-actor, like a benched player, and they absolutely refused to have anything to do with it. Look at breakfast, it is thrown in with your hotel stay as the breakfast buffet, tagged on as part of the price of your bed for the night. What we did is that we took an understudy and gave it a small stage; we gave it lights, we gave it music, and we turned it into a Broadway production on Orchard Road. We did not have a lunch menu; we did not have a dinner menu; we did not have a separate menu. It was the same menu throughout the day, with no pasta, no pizza, and no burgers. We never wanted to be something for everybody. We wanted to be the place for people who loved eating breakfast. If I had listened to industry experts, I would have been swayed from my original idea, but I always stuck to my guns on the all-day breakfast concept. Conviction is so important in business.

Authenticity

Does food need to be authentic? Who decides what is authentic? There are a thousand ways to cook an egg. So which way is correct? From the outset, I was clear. We would cook according to the Singaporean taste. We could do this because we were going to do everything by ourselves, everything would be inhouse, and that would set us apart. Allan Benton of Benton's Country Hams fame once said, 'You'll always lose when you play someone else's game.'

Wild Honey was going to tell our story, showing how we LOVED breakfast. I feel very strongly that Wild Honey was successful because we were able to tweak international food to Singaporean tastes. The brilliance of this was, if you know how people like to eat and the flavours they enjoy, it becomes less foreign, more familiar, and they come back for more. So, we opened the way forward by making it delicious for Singaporeans. All of the extensive research that we did was critical. We had invited our Singaporean neighbours and friends on weekends for tastings. They would give us feedback from a Singaporean perspective. This preparation was very important because it gave us the confidence that the food that we were cooking was going down well, so that when we finally opened on 27 November, we were ready to go. There's a big difference between the readiness—we already knew how to measure things and portioning—versus the quality of the product: flavours and presentation, which was what we needed—to be prepared for our local market—for the actual opening.

Processes

Getting the final product to the customer is a big responsibility and a stressful task in any restaurant. Who decides when food is ready to be served? How many people do you seat at the same time? I am a control freak when it comes to dining room service. The Guest Relations Officer (GRO), which is the politically correct name for what was formerly named *hostess* in Singapore, is the first line of defence. She will make eye contact at a distance of about five metres and extend a greeting when you are three metres away. Yes, every time. Once you are checked in, just like for a hotel room, the second GRO, the sitter, will escort you to the table. They will present the menu and explain the daily specials. If you need to charge your phone or dry your umbrella, she will assist you. Child seat? Not a problem. Colouring books and pencils? Yes we have plenty of those for the children. Table not stable? She will place a rubber door stopper underneath. If the guest is cold, we will offer a scarf or a pillow for a pregnant lady. If the guest is dining alone, we will offer glossy magazines. Once the table is checked-in, it goes from confirmed status (gold) to seated (orange). The restaurant management software will inform us after 120 minutes by turning red, and that means time to go. So, the dining experience is designed to last two hours, and we found over time that by providing free internet for two hours, our guest could enjoy the entire dining experience within those two hours.

Once orders are taken, they go directly to the bar and kitchen. The preparation time for drinks is five to ten minutes, depending on the recipe. The kitchen is divided into the hot kitchen, the cold section, and the pastry area. So, when the head chef calls for a ticket to be prepared, the team must time each station to prep the order. The tickets come fast and hard, and we easily feed over 500 guests a day, and this makes the task of efficient food delivery paramount. If the food arrives before the drinks, then we have a problem at the bar. If snacks arrive before hot food, then it is a problem on the hotline. Our standard is to complete each table by serving children first, then adults. However, different items of food have different cooking times. Cold food tends to be faster than well done proteins. Some dishes are served with French fries which cool down quickly. Some guests require sauce on the side or other special requests. Not only does the head chef need to remember everything, but he must also communicate the orders verbally to all the stations. This is Singapore, so some cooks are Chinese, some Indian, some Malay. I demand that all orders are spoken in English and become very nasty when people in my kitchens ignore this very important ethos. Kitchens are called brigades, like in the army, because *La Brigade de cuisine* applies a military chain of command to the kitchen, with a clear delegation of roles aimed at encouraging efficiency, precision, and a sense of high urgency. Most western kitchens function in a brigade system developed by the legendary Master Chef Auguste Escoffier. He would tie the brigade together with strings and drill them on mobility and technique. During Covid-19, I was so unhappy with my kitchen, I actually tied the kitchen brigade together around the waist and made them go left and right by shouting commands through a video. It was a very sobering lesson for them. Kitchens are hot and stressful rooms. This energy can turn into positive stress, like an athlete before a competition, or can be like a rock band before performing for a huge crowd, where screaming can lead to chaos and confusion. The turnover is very high in staffing; it is physical work on your feet all day, and many restaurants fail because they cannot hire, train, and motivate their kitchen staff.

Everything in Wild Honey is made inhouse with love, from the Hollandaise sauce (with a dash of tabasco for spice) to the ajvar, dukkha, schug, hummus, guacamole, jams, sponge cakes, scones, creme patisserie, buttermilk pancake batter, granola, and waffle batter. This requires tremendous organization and procurement skills. I am a strong believer that any missing item is a loss of sales. If the chef does not order in time, then Wild Honey runs out. Some items are imported from overseas, so they require more lead time, whilst others are stored offsite. For example, we buy sturgeon fish from France (yes, it is farmed). It arrives in a frozen container and lasts for around one year. Our supplier of fine food stores it for us. Wild Honey is highly specialized and requires exotic spices and ingredients from around the world. Order too much and you risk wastage as storage space is limited and so is the shelf life of organic food. Once the food arrives, it must be peeled, chopped, diced, grated, cooked, and cooled down. Then, it must be chilled under temperature-controlled conditions in a holding area and then labelled. Through the years, our procurement practices have become more effective and professional. In order to get more involved in this process, we engaged the services of a company called Food-Razor, a Singapore start-up, whose technology allows us to follow price changes, product changes, timelines and accounting from a control panel. It meant that I could view any of the three restaurants we had then, at any time from my computer. So my first question when I come to work is, 'Anything missing on the menu?' My next comment is, 'Housekeeping'. I use those two words throughout the day both in the back and front of the house. I recently appointed a chief steward to address that priority in every outlet. He functions as housekeeping, goods-receiver, and also takes month end inventory. Most suppliers are honest and dependable, however they are only human and can easily make a mistake. For example, recently we added a Korean salad which included a gluten free soy sauce ingredient. The supplier ran out and replaced that bottle with another brand that had gluten. How did we know? One of our guests fell sick and informed us. These things happen, so we have to always remain vigilant.

Once the food is plated, the food expediter needs to remember they must check the food against the ticket and not forget any special request like takeaway. I will refuse to take a plate from any station without getting a ticket in my hand. It is my way of showing the kitchen that I know what is going on and to check the alertness of the station. I suffer from short-term memory loss and I joke by calling it mad cow disease, so I insist on everything in writing. The white ticket goes to the kitchen, and the yellow ticket goes to the food runner; they are the octopi with many hands that reach every table. They will inform the chef when a table is ready to fire (pick up) the next course. Running a restaurant is like an orchestra, the chef is the conductor and the first violin is the maître d'. They must listen to every instrument and keep everyone's pulse, not too fast, not too slow. The food delivery will mirror the seating rhythm every time. It is a tango, and the best restaurants create magic in this concert hall.

No substitutions

At Wild Honey, we have a no substitution policy. We had limited space in the first shop, and we felt the priority was to maintain our rhythm and flow. Many people perceived this as inflexible and arrogant, but again I stuck to my guns. The media had a field day with this but consistency is very hard to achieve in any restaurant, and I knew substitutions would impact our quality. So, I needed to be fair to the kitchen. If the culinary standards were not clear, then we could not define delicious and gauge what was a success. We needed a clear understanding of how the dishes would be cooked, plated, and presented to the guest. This was a marker I was not willing to move for anyone and never did. Until today, we do not make any kind of substitutions and our regulars know how to order off the menu. Most people do not cook, so why would we take culinary direction from them? Well done poached eggs? No. Less spicy Tunisian? No. This dish is made from fresh tomatoes, chillies, onions, and paprika, and cooked in a large pot every day, so when people ask for less spicy, we cannot take the spice out of our Tunisian. The guiding principle for every dish is that the main ingredient cannot be removed. Would you want to watch a Broadway musical without the star of the show? In our Flinders Lane, we do not remove the middle eastern pancake called malawach because it is the star. We cook our scrambled eggs in cream and butter, and they are whisked with air to make the eggs light, but some people request olive oil which changes the flavour dramatically. So, which way should we go? Do we do it our way or keep changing our standards to please people? We should stick to the things we do best. We cannot please everybody, and those companies that do try to, they lose direction and motivation because it is not their story anymore. Pizza, pasta, salad bar, rice dishes, pastries, noodles—these are some of the suggestions we gladly ignored over the years. A good menu is like a good playlist—some old songs mixed with the newbies.

Wild Honey was never going to rely on a chef to develop the dishes, and because neither Stephanie nor I are chefs, we had our own unique approach. Given the perennial issues I would face with chefs, we would not have survived any other way.

Wild Honey Recipes

In the early days, I was very protective of our recipes and would never have dreamed of sharing them. Besides, our recipes changed because our goal was to encourage the dishes we knew from our childhoods to evolve with new ingredients and interactions. The recipes collected over the years came from many sources including cookbooks, food magazines, family recipes, and our travels around the world. Gradually, we found other cafes were copying our recipes. I was shocked, both by the fact that people were taking our cooking seriously and also that anyone would choose imitation as a strategy, a guaranteed path to mediocrity in my view. Still, one of the most frequent questions we receive in Wild Honey is how we cook our food. By 2018, we felt it was a good idea to document our signature dishes by way of curating our first cookbook. We were ready to share the joy.

In the restaurant, our recipes are documented in an application called ShopNCook. This includes costing and nutritional information based on the USDA nutrient database. Stephanie was the lead on this cookbook project. First, she needed to convert the portioning from batch recipe to domestic portioning, which was easier said than done. We had high resolution pictures of most of the dishes, but some needed to be retaken. It was difficult to choose which dishes we would include in the book, but we decided to focus on our egg dishes. We researched other cookbooks like *Bill's* by Chef Bill Granger from Sydney. His genius is making recipes idiotproof so even people like me can use them. Stephanie is an avid collector of his books. Another source of inspiration was the Palamar cookbook from London. We wanted people to enjoy our recipes by cooking them in their own kitchens. If you would like to cook with us, order our cookbook from our website at www.wildhoney.com.sg.

Partnerships

We have immense respect for strong brands, thus another critical aspect of our development was tying up with some of these brands. This was one of the reasons we began working with the iconic TWG company. Quality was our foundation, and in an all-day breakfast restaurant, good quality tea and coffee were essential. Our problem however was not tea quality but that our baristas were not trained properly in tea preparation and tea service. This created a lack of consistency and quality in our tea programme as good tea requires precision. We needed outside expertise, and since Stephanie was a big fan of TWG, she recommended that we approach them. TWG, founded by a Moroccan French husband-and-wife team, was the quintessential combination of quality and branding. Mr Taha Bouqdib built up his experience working as a tea sommelier in Paris, and on arriving in Singapore in 2007, partnered with the local Singaporean businessman Manoj Murjani, a Hong Kong resident of Indian descent. Their vision was to create a new lifestyle luxury brand for Asia around tea. They founded TWG with a start-up capital of US $10 million and in less than three years made their money back. Taha cultivated strong relationships with tea growers, and this resulted in the sourcing of China's prized Da Hong Pao tea belonging to the Oolong family and grown in the Wuyi mountains in Northern Fujian province. Due to its rarity prior to 2005, the tea leaves were reserved for the Chinese government, but the relaxing of those rules was a huge opportunity that he was able to cash in on. Thanks to TWG, the Chinese now travel to Singapore to buy the world's most expensive tea to take back to China. Reverse on reverse. In a country known for swift production, the emphasis on quality and luxury packaging would make it difficult for the Chinese to replicate this brand. Ingenious. The emphasis was on affordable luxury, and it was aiming at Asia as the fastest growing market in the world. In fact, an aggressive wholesale strategy saw the China segment quickly account for above 40 per cent of the total revenue. It was a low risk–high exposure approach that landed TWG in every Starwood property in China.

In Singapore, the first salon opened in 2008 in the central business district at Republic Plaza and became profitable the following year. Many doubted that tea would sell in Asia as the joke was that in Asia, tea is free! Adding to this, 2008 was an economic crisis, so it was a bold move to open then. To encourage people to understand the product, the company created books to help customers appreciate the origins and history of the teas on sale. It also created several tea-related accessories, and this is where the tie-up with Wild Honey came in. In 2014, as part of its efforts to inculcate a tea drinking culture in Singapore, TWG Tea opened a training facility at its headquarters to train tea sommeliers. Wild Honey was the first restaurant in the world to receive certification from the TWG training academy. For Wild Honey, the education of our tea butlers, the tea menu, hardware and expertise have helped our tea sales triple. This is another example of how seriously we take staff training. Today, TWG has 3,000 employees worldwide and by 2017 had twelve stores in Singapore, totalling US $90 million in revenue. With seventy stores across nineteen countries, it makes several hundred million every year. We do love a success story.

Of course, quality tea is nothing without an equally quality coffee. Our partnership with Common Man Coffee Roasters has been critical to the experience we provide at Wild Honey. Another Singapore brand, this one was the brainchild of Cynthia Chan from the Esprit Group, till then known for her finesse in the field of selfcare and beauty, and Harry Glover of Forty Hands Café. Importing beans from Brazil, Mexico, Sumatra, and India, to name a few places, they create their own blends. When they opened their first outlet on Robinson Road, it housed a coffee academy. Once again, our barista training was taken care of. They trained them in skills like grinding, temperature control, micro-foaming, and, of course, latte art. CMCR creates our unique Wild Honey blend seasonally and even sponsored our first two handmade coffee machines from Seattle, SENSYO. This was no small gesture on their part as this was the Maserati of Coffee Machines.

Fine tea and fine coffee and fine food. Our strategic partnership with Culina has been critical to the quality of fare our customers receive. Since we opened in 2009, we have partnered with Culina, the brainchild of Christina Ong, the powerhouse behind the Como group, to obtain all our premium meats, sustainable farmed fish, and old and new world wines. They are artisanal suppliers that craft distinctive and sustainable food in a manner steeped in tradition, and to have a provider committed to such a high level of quality was another critical partnership for us.

Social Media

In 2020, Wild Honey was once again awarded the Best Cafe in Singapore by Chope. I know this was in no small part due to our social media presence, which has played an integral role in sustaining and promoting our brand. My experiences on social media were not positive. I do not have an Instagram account. I respectfully left social media to Stephanie. I did not foresee its significance and also found the interaction with negative postings extremely stressful. We are active on Instagram and Facebook, as apart from in the restaurant itself, this is the primary means of communication with our customers. We definitely remain ahead of the curve, posting everyday as well as updating Insta stories. Social media today is the word-of-mouth of past years, and Stephanie rode that wave early.

In fact, the beauty of social media is that much of this content is generated by excited customers who shoot and post. In Asia, taking a picture of your food on a mobile telephone is almost a prerequisite to the experience, so 80 per cent of our content is generated by our customers. Pictures of our food is obviously the staple content, but over time, because our venues have evolved, social media posts have reflected that change through increasing posts of children (we are very kid friendly) and now dogs (our newest outlet South Beach welcomes pets). This is a carefully managed and curated aspect of our business with strict protocols. When we repost pictures of children, we ask for permission. When we repost pictures of food in which we have been generously tagged, we always credit the original poster. We promote our specials and events through social media. You would be surprised at the number of guests who walk in and show us an image from social media and request the exact dish that they have an image of on their mobile phone, which means that we have to be sure what is posted is still on the menu because we do not want to disappoint! As important as online bookings systems are (and they are integral to the business), nothing speaks to a customer louder than personal responses on social media. The most common question we get asked is—can I make a reservation? We reply to messages within 24 hours, and people are so grateful for this personal interaction. This type of attention provides an authenticity that Stephanie understood very early on would distinguish Wild Honey from its competitors.

Social media allows us to acknowledge the value of our customers. We have about 40,000 subscribers in our database built up through our Chope reservation system and Wi-Fi logins at the restaurant. If they have kindly left us an email address and birth month, we send them customized mails asking if they would like to celebrate their birthday with us, and we offer a free slice of cake. Social media and direct communication also mean that disgruntled and dissatisfied customers can make feedback heard loud and clear. Stephanie and our media specialist, Sabine handle this with an openness and generosity I would not be able to. They view bad reviews as constructive, an opportunity to learn and improve, and they reply to each and everyone. They never want customers to feel like they are shouting into a void and will reach out offline to unhappy customers, to engage with them directly, and address their concerns.

During Covid-19, our social media posts became even more important for keeping in touch with our customers. Interactions increased to daily, and message content changed to engage more with the serious issues confronting Singaporeans. Our business model had also changed to delivery-only, and being so active on social media, the message got to our customers instantaneously.

Stephanie took the radical decision of changing our link on Wild Honey's Instagram bio to our third-party island-wide delivery provider to put delivery front and centre.

Trust is another pillar of success that has been strengthened by our social media presence. Gradually, people want to see the people behind the brand, and this became even more critical during the pandemic. Customers wanted to know who was behind the brand. Were we trustworthy? It had begun with the trust that we would evolve and cater to them, vegetarian, vegan, gluten free, children, and now dogs, but increasingly with the pandemic, reaching out to our customers to build trust became more urgent. Initially, we shied away from publicity, preferring the brand and the quality to speak for itself, but the longer we stayed in business and expanded, the harder it has been to stay out of the limelight. Today, when a direct mail goes to our customers, it is personally written by Steph, the font is cursive, emulating a handwritten script, and it is signed by us, Stephanie and Guy.

Chapter 13

No Reservations, Please

So, back to the story now: After nine months of frantic preparations, it was finally Wild Honey's opening day.

On Friday, 27 November 2009, Jimmy and I arrived at 8 a.m. not knowing what to expect. We found a few people waiting for us to open. It was wonderful and humbling, and some of the panic of the last months was alleviated. I remember one of our first guests was the general manager of the Mandarin Meritus Catherine Wong, who came to wish us luck and pay us our first dollar bills. I quickly turned on the music, lights, and air conditioning while Jimmy changed into his chef's uniform and switched the gas pilots on. Bread was baked, and by 9 a.m. we had a line of people waiting at the door. I personally greeted every guest and instructed them to order at the counter with me. To our relief, by 10 a.m., more staff had arrived, but ordering was becoming an issue. I had decided that at Wild Honey, you would order at the counter and not at the table, but it was clear that people were confused whether to order first or choose their table and then order. I noted to myself that a guest relations officer would be needed to greet, explain the flow, and seat the guests. That Friday was a smashing success with 201 covers. It was mind boggling. All the supplies in the kitchen were finished, and Jimmy then prepped all night so that we would be ready for Saturday. We were hitting the ground running.

Very quickly, the word about Wild Honey spread like wildfire. Normally in a restaurant printer paper rolls are changed once a day, but we were flying through them. However, we did not take reservations, and we discovered that the volume on weekends was particularly high, so we needed a better way to manage the waiting guests. We offered complimentary coffee and Irish tea bread. People appreciated this effort. For us, this was personal, we remembered names and faces and worked the door old school with pen and paper. I was trained by some of New York's best maître d's to maximize seating, and I used every trick in the book. What choice did I have? I had created the demand for our fifty seats, so now I needed to supply the goods. We had created something very unique and original—all-day breakfast on the Singapore High Street. I think creating that demand for Wild Honey's all-day breakfast was our biggest success because that is the biggest challenge for any new business.

We were working out the processes as we went along, and I was flying by the seat of my pants. There was a danger of people ordering without a table, so we decided to seat guests first and then instruct them to order from the counter. The whole process needed a gentle hand. Someone to guide our keen and hungry guests seamlessly through the system. I recalled meeting Andreas' wife Saraswati, a beautiful Indian woman, and she seemed like the right person to do this. Saras became our lead guest relations officer, and the guests loved her warmth and charm. It was very satisfying to see so many returning guests who appreciated the energy and vibe of Wild Honey.

The seater's job was to screen every table and make predictions based on allocated time, but this is not possible without reservations; so, I needed to guess how long each guest would take. This made the waiting time unpredictable, and during peak hours, people usually waited under half an hour, but sometimes it was longer. Many people requested making reservations, but we declined; it was strictly first come, first served. Keep it simple, I thought, but we had got cult status, and the lines got longer, and it became more difficult to manage the hungry, grumpy diners. After forty-five minutes of waiting, disappointment turned into frustration then into anger.

One Saturday, a family of three was extremely upset because they thought we had cut the line for a friend. We had not, and as it turned out that table that we were accused of giving away was actually for the complaining woman's boss. Talk about an unfortunate coincidence for her. Her boss got involved in the fracas and it all became very embarrassing for her. Probably not the best of career moves for her. Why did Wild Honey make people so aggressive and crazy? What was the solution? Our staff became uncomfortable handling seating during peak periods, which was a huge red flag to me. Unhappy staff was a recipe for destruction.

* * *

As encouraging as it was to have queues, we desperately needed to find a system that would not alienate our clientele with the continually long frustrating waits. Technology once again came to the rescue. Tic Toc was a huge help to us, not the video sharing system that is the latest millennial trend, but the local start-up managing queuing systems developed by a local entrepreneur, Lee Jun Kian. The system worked with the guests keying in their names and numbers and then they were given an electronic number via SMS. They were then free to browse the mall and shop. When the table was ready, the guest relations officer, Saras, would send them a message notifying them to approach the hostess stand.

This technology was a huge help for our guest relations team, improved flow, and reduced the tension and fear created by the huge lines on the weekends and public holidays. Best of all, it remembered guest details for future visits, which meant we could keep a record and get in touch with them again.

The payment method also needed to be efficient. The point-of-sale system I was using was Micros Fidelio, and it responded well to my key-ins, it was simple and effective. Another innovation was a payment gateway by Standard Chartered bank which allowed us to swipe the guests card to settle via terminal—remember this was ten years before payWave—and, thankfully, this allowed payments to be fast. I was surprised by how much cash was being used by customers. Many wealthy Indonesian guests would pay with thousand-dollar notes, so I would need to run to the hotel cashier to break the big notes. Some paid with Brunei dollars, which was fine in Singapore, but some wanted to pay with USD, and we directed them to the money changers on Orchard Road. These were good problems to have, and we were prepared. However, our pay-at-the counter system was not popular because it meant queuing first to order, which not many Singaporeans were used to and so there was resistance to it.

One day, Stephanie was helping me run things when a couple walked in. They refused to order at the counter and made a huge scene. Stephanie was upset. Why did people behave like this in a public place? What made them think it was correct to treat people in the service industry this way? In New York, if you behaved badly in a respectable restaurant, you would be given the exit sign, but here in Singapore some of the guests whistled, snapped fingers, pointed, and used vulgarities. This was a real culture shock for us. Luckily, it was only a very small percentage of our guests. By focusing on our regulars, we kept upbeat and always tried to stay positive.

We started getting reviewed, but even the positive reviews had issues with our payment system. We were heartened when just a month after opening, *The Business Times* published a lively little review in its 'Dining' section. It appeared on Christmas Day 2009 no less, but it had a caveat. Jaime Ee wrote: 'There are several reasons why you would want to eat breakfast at 4 p.m. in the afternoon, or even in the evening: (a) You have a very bad hangover, (b) It is technically breakfast time in London or New York, (c) Finally, there is a restaurant where the staff do not coldly tell you "We stop serving breakfast at 10:30 a.m." Wild Honey is one of those rare eateries that take an old concept, make it new and yet familiar enough to make diners wonder why no one thought of it before opening yet another burger joint.' Then came the kicker: 'The only kink in the charming armour is its unfriendly ordering system. You have to order and pay at the counter, which gets fiddly, especially if there is a bunch of people arriving at the same time. Once you have made your order, the wait staff will serve you at your table. If you want dessert after, they will take your order at your table. Which does not really make sense, so one hopes that Wächs tweaks things to offer full table service. Whether he does or does not, he has already got a hit on his hands. Breakfast is the most important meal of the day—now it can be the favourite meal, any time of day.'

The Straits Times, on the other hand, was positively offended by our system. In the 'Life' section on Saturday, 20 February 2010 by Rebecca Lynne Tan, the headline read 'Queue to order but still a service charge'. She compared Wild Honey to a hawker centre and encouraged readers to voice their opinions with CASE, the consumer association of Singapore. She wrote: 'Do you think that pay-at-the-counter restaurants should levy a service charge?' In my interview with her, I replied, 'The focus should be about the food and the service, not about the payment process. By getting the payment process out of the way with speed and accuracy, we eliminate the whole of waiting for the bill and waving the server down.'

Wild Honey was, in fact, ten years ahead of its time. Today, contactless payments are the new normal in F&B retail; it is faster, safer, and more accurate. Although Wild Honey was not flexible like other restaurants and although it was true that we did not offer a menu at the table, we did offer hostess services, water, cooked and served food, prepared and served beverages, and cleaned tables, which, to me, meant service. So, we decided to continue to improve service rather than cancel service charge, which was intended for the staff, but in Singapore, for some reason, did not go directly to them. I think it should and serve as a motivator for better service.

We closed 2009 with a bang.

Chapter 14

One Million Dollars

Before opening, I had been given the advice to ignore profit and loss. How scary is that for a new business owner? It turns out it was one of the most valuable pieces of advice I have been given. So, I focused on the top line, delivered on the service, and ignored my financials for the first year. It was an incredibly hard thing for me to do, but I did it. When you open a business, there are a lot of distractions, and if you can ignore the P&L, you have the tunnel vision to just focus on the work. I focused on Wild Honey sixteen hours a day, seven days a week, dedicating my best work to it. In an owner-driven enterprise, if people can see you, they know that you will be there, and they rely on it.

I was completely immersed in the day-to-day, Stephanie and Alex hardly saw me, I was losing weight, chain smoking, and had become very edgy. I was so determined to make sure that Wild Honey delivered on its promise, I had ignored the bottom line, and, within a year, it had paid off. Then, lo and behold, would you believe it, one day Stephanie texted me and said, 'Congratulations, you are a millionaire. You have hit your first million.' I nearly fell down in disbelief. Business was booming.

In restaurants, the danger of disappointing guests on a second experience is very real. The night before opening, we had a friend visiting us from London. His name was John

Ritchie, and he asked me what I wished for. Success, I said. John warned me that success can be a double-edged sword. He told us a story about a neighbourhood restaurant in London where he had been a regular. It was John's favourite place. One day, the food critic from *The Financial Times* reviewed the restaurant and gave it a high rating, overnight the business volume doubled, the staff could not take the pressure, and the whole place fell apart. Finding out about our first million reminded me of this story.

* * *

The problem with hospitality is that it demands total commitment with no mercy and no time for anything else. I needed to give up some control and learn to trust my team. I became increasingly aware that I needed to find a strong assistant, especially with Stephanie still working fulltime at JWT. I was introduced to David Rogers through Tobias Busse, my good old friend in New York. He had an interesting background, American born, educated in Cornell's Master School of Hospitality, and then recruited by McDonald's for their executive team for North America. After that, he studied ashtanga yoga in India, became a yogi, and opened up a yoga studio in New Mexico. David had come to Singapore and had been teaching yoga in True Yoga. We met, and I had a good feeling about working together with him. He would become my Spock from Star Trek. Calculated, wise, and unemotional. David accepted the position a few months after the opening of Wild Honey.

The first thing David had to do was tackle my inability to delegate. He explained that by allowing people to learn from their own mistakes, they would grow. This concept was very hard for me to swallow because mistakes cost money. Still, he was telling me that mistakes are good and that I should be happy because it meant that my staff would learn. It sounded like some hippy wishful thinking to me, but David was right. I had been so busy getting everything else ready that I had not focused enough on staff training. I needed help with creating a real work culture that would encourage the love of food, being of service, and entertaining people. I had learned during my hotel training in Brenners Park-Hotel in Baden-Baden that preparation would be key and the brand experience was all important. From the first interaction on our website, landline, the elevators, the entrance, greetings, ordering, seating; these were touch points that could make or break the experience of visiting Wild Honey. With the first year under my belt, I had to focus on maintaining the high standards.

In 2012, I found Anitha Tan and May Ho from Sage Training through my contact Victor, who was the president of the Coffee Association of Singapore. They specialized in staff training, loved the idea of working with Wild Honey, and the chemistry was right. Being experts in their field, they understood the service challenges we faced each day. Together, we focused on communication, body language, leadership, troubleshooting, and motivation as the keys to training our staff successfully. For example, one session consisted of filming our staff walking on a catwalk and analysing how their walk sent a message of confidence versus uncertainty. They learned how to stand straight and balance a book on their head. Both May and Anitha had the pedigree for butler service. May had been a cabin crew for Singapore Airlines, and Anitha had worked at the Four Seasons Singapore as the human resources manager. I joined in and used my certification from the Court of Master Sommeliers to teach my staff skills like balancing trays, measuring and pouring champagne into flutes, then moving gracefully around the dining room.

I remember an old interview on 60 Minutes covering Chef Thomas Keller from The French Laundry, where he talked about paying a ballet teacher to instruct his service staff on dancing in the dining room. Genius. After all, what is dining if not theatre all around? People want to be entertained. Not only are our service staff sales staff, but they also need to be entertainers. Knowing when to converse with a guest is a skill that takes years to cultivate. Subjects may include current events, sports, fashion, popular culture, travel, but it should never become too personal. Asking a guest for a photo or their number is strictly forbidden at Wild Honey. One day, we had the host of *Asia Got Talent* as a guest and my guest relations officer requested a photo with them. It reminded me of a young Guy Wächs trying to get Lou Reed's autograph many years earlier. I gave her a strong warning. Privacy is golden and protecting the personal information of our guests is paramount.

* * *

I tried to bring some New York culture to Singapore. The restaurant only had fifty seats including eight bar stools. Even though the stools had a nice view looking down on Orchard Road, they had no backrest, and most people wanted their own table. Many restaurants look at dining in even numbers, however these side stools were very useful for our odd numbers. There is a myth that single diners spend less, but I found that the opposite was true. They spent more because they treated themselves. I remember when I was working at Cafe Centro in New York, my charming boss Renaud Ammon would always offer a complimentary glass of champagne to women who were dining alone. He had such class, but then, of course, he was French. In Wild Honey, we offer magazines and other surprises to women to make them feel comfortable.

When addressing a couple, I will make contact with the lady first, when serving the food, we try to serve the lady first whenever possible. If a lady has a handbag, we will offer a small stool to place it on. Even the lighting in Wild Honey complimented the woman—warm, subtle, and intimate.

While we were ironing out the kinks, our restaurant was getting attention. That first positive review in *The Straits Times* after our pre-event faded into the background, it felt like a lifetime ago. I know I am supposed to welcome feedback, I know there is always room for improvement, and I know not being noticed is worse than criticism. Still, some of the feedback felt like gut punches. Wild Honey was a labour of love, a creative process that was very personal, and, at this stage, I was still fragile and uncertain at times.

A popular publication, in 2010, had issues from the get-go with our concept. Not only were they unimpressed with all day breakfast they found our decor too bohemian and unoriginal. Their review of our food was a bit hit and miss—some food items hit the mark like our perennial favourite dish, the Tunisian, but others did not.

Ouch—it did hurt but then some of it was fair.

They were not impressed with our decor either. 'And upon entering the cozy little space on the third floor of Mandarin Gallery, the second niggle is how transparently derivative it all is. The interiors owe much to P.S. Cafe's DNA, it shares the same dark timber flooring and mismatched retro furniture, comfy armchairs, and low-slung tables, right down to a small wall rack of reading material including *The New Yorker*, *Monocle*, *Wallpaper*, *Esquire*, and *Rolling Stone*.' So, they hated the concept and found our space unoriginal.

The review of the food was a bit hit and miss: 'Its dishes do not feel too obvious like breakfast.' The Italian was praised for being 'flavourful and textbook perfect in its creamy texture' but they felt 'it was a raw deal that you were not getting what you thought you were ordering, which was a frittata.' Our perennial favourite dish, the Tunisian, passed the test. It was 'a lovely pan of sunny side up eggs lounging in a tomato stew that was punched through with chorizo, it felt so comforting to mop up the molten lot with the brioche.'

The pricing passed, but only just. 'For what you are paying an average of $35 per head, the portions are not particularly large, but to the kitchen's credit, everything is prepared with unusually seasoned aplomb.'

The biggest challenge in Singapore, then and today, is service. There we took a hammering. 'Where Wild Honey really trips is with its inexperienced wait staff. Our orders needed to be repeated three times. Orders were delivered to the wrong tables. Serving plates arrived wet. Coming back to the table after placing my dessert order at the counter, I found that my three-quarter full glass of lovely, thirst-quenching nature remedy had been cleared away. When I brought this up, the response was, "Would you like to order another one?" The waitress's helpful suggestion was met with a stony silence. "Never mind, never mind! I'll make another one for you," she said hurriedly. You think?'

Ouch.

Nevertheless, criticism aside, Wild Honey became the place to go for a date, anniversary, birthday, reunion, or just to have fun. People wrote us beautiful letters about how much they loved Wild Honey. Some people even drove from Kuala Lumpur and Johor Bahru just to eat at Wild Honey. The Sultan of Brunei, the owner of the Hyatt Singapore, came. Raj Kumar of Royal Brothers loved the concept so much that he offered me a joint venture in one of his many properties in Singapore. His is an entrepreneurial success story if there ever was one. Starting his career buying a tailor shop in Lucky

Plaza, he then bought all the shops until he owned the mall. Since then, Royal Brothers has become a huge developer worldwide. His offer was a big thumbs up to us.

Most of our guests were friendly and considerate, but we did have some bad apples. On one occasion, a Mr RT claimed that he was discriminated against and was given a bad table because he was a Singaporean. He launched a campaign on Singapore's Stomp website, accusing me of being an American pig who hated Asians. I was so hurt. As a Jew who had worked in New York, I had Pakistani, French, Thai, Mexican, Irish, Bangladeshi, African, and Moroccan colleagues in the restaurant industry. Racism was just not accepted in hospitality; we are a diverse and open industry. The situation deteriorated when I replied to him publicly on Facebook. It was a big mistake, and only made the situation worse. Stephanie and I were feeling sick about the attacks, and we did not know how to make what felt like a nightmare go away. We could not figure out what was behind such pure hate. Was it from a competitor? An ex-employee trying to get even? We even ended up hiring a PR firm to draft a response. After four long weeks, it finally stopped. It was then that I realized the true power of social media: that it could be used as a weapon against business owners and that the internet was the wild west with no rules or morality.

When we opened Wild Honey, I believed that Facebook and Twitter were just the flavour of the year and would go away. I was born in 1971, so my first experience with computers was in grade 12 back in 1988. With the internet, it was in 1995 when the first web browser came out. In those days, you needed to dial in using a landline. Try explaining that to your millennial child. By the time I opened my Facebook account as late as 2004, I realized that I could not have been more wrong about the relevance of social media. I had no idea how information technology and social media were going to change people's behaviour and eating trends. This was even before smartphones, so computers were really the only go-to to find out the latest trends. You could be the best restaurant in the world, but if that was not reflected in marketing and social media, people would question your success. That one experience was enough for me, and I never went near it again. Stephanie manages Wild Honey's social media, and I have stopped reading reviews. I am on the ground, and I listen to the customers. Between the two of us, I think we cover it all.

That year, Wild Honey won the Epicurus Top Ten Award for best restaurant, 2010. Steph and I felt very proud.

Chapter 15

Expansion

Still, this was all coming at a cost. I was not spending any time with my family. The pressure of staff shortages, long hours, and taking work home with me was pushing me over the edge. It also took its toll on Chef Jimmy. The pressure on the kitchen was so high that he was burned out. After just twelve months, he resigned. He never cooked again and went on to successfully sell ovens for Manotech. We are still friends today. This became the first of a Wild Honey trend; I could never keep a chef.

When Chef Jimmy resigned, I was completely unprepared, a mistake I would try and avoid going forward. In fact, I was unprepared for the whole staffing issue in Singapore because in Europe and in the United States, finding service staff had never been an issue. I decided to promote his assistant Chuan Thomas as head Chef, whilst our pastry chef would remain the same. We also hired a Filipino, Jesse, as a line cook. He was hardworking and performed to our satisfaction even though he did not have a culinary education. However, we made the mistake of using a shady recruitment agency to find Jesse, and, as it turned out, they were not very careful with verifying the papers of their recruits. This would come back to bite me later.

Another creative move was turning our second steward from China into a prep cook. Improvization is the single most effective skill in F&B retail. Flexibility, adaptability, and troubleshooting became our mantra at Wild Honey, especially in an industry where staffing could even have a daily turnover. It was sad for me to see Jimmy leave. I wanted to grow together and help him become a partner, but that is life, and he moved on.

* * *

There were many hiccups that first year. In retrospect, it was natural. One of my first mistakes when we opened was not signing an agreement letter directly with American Express. I learned about payment systems the hard way. American Express disputed our first week of Amex transactions, which was not a small sum of $5,000, because we had used Standard Chartered as our banking merchant. I explained that as far as I understood, by signing with Standard Chartered, I had covered Amex, but they declined to honour the payments. An expensive mistake for a start-up, and for this reason, I declined Amex for ten years. It was only after we became cashless in 2020 that we finally moved on and signed with Amex. The results have been good and some of our regular guests were delighted to be able to finally use their Kris Flyer cards. I could learn from these setbacks, but staffing was, and still is, a perennial issue for the service industry in Singapore. I truly believe that if anything will be our undoing, it will be staffing problems.

The F&B scene in Singapore was changing fast and furiously, and in the midst of our first year, Singapore's first integrated resort Marina Bay Sands opened. This was a major milestone for tourism in Singapore and lifted the service standards and entertainment quality in F&B retail to a whole new level. Sands cost US $5.5 billion to build and opened their doors on 23 June 2010. It was a massive endeavour, designed by the world famous Israeli designer Moshe Safdie. It had huge MICE facilities, a casino, and over 2,000 hotel rooms. The grand opening boasted a spectacular light and water show at the ArtScience Museum and dominated Singapore's landscape with its distinctive boat-suspended-on-two-pillars design.

MBS set the new gold standard for retail luxury and high-end F&B with concepts imported from around the world. The standards of restaurants in the city were being raised exponentially. The vice president in charge of F&B was an astute choice. Tamir Shanhel was a seasoned operator from Las Vegas, a visionary and charming to boot, and he convinced some of the biggest names in F&B retail to open their first shops in Singapore. Their approach had three key components: managed and owned (Rise), celebrity chefs and leased retail outlets, which had a lower risk and higher chances of success. The celebrity chefs were chosen by Shanhel and his team and the capital expenditure for the celebrity chefs was financed wholly by MBS. The Singapore Tourism Board was involved in the initial proposal of choosing the celebrity chefs, but they were ultimately chosen based on their track records and thereafter had total creative freedom in design, concept, menu, and operations. Basically, they ran independently from the hotel and the integrated resort. The celebrity chefs were very hands-on and only depended on the main kitchen of the hotel for certain products.

Another consideration was placing fast food Asian restaurants inside the integrated resort, as this was also a necessary component. Tamir created amazing events like the launch of the MBS inaugural Epicurean Market in 2013, a three-day gourmet food and wine appreciation event. Later, he set up the World Gourmet Summit, which introduced ordinary people to fine dining by selling bite sized portions in a market environment in the specially set up convention centre. This three-day event took place every year between 2015 and

2018 and proved to be a culinary orgasm for food lovers. Tamir also hired a director of wine who created the best wine cave in Asia, holding the most expensive wines in the world. It was all a wonderful addition to the scene and resulted in a spate of celebrity chef restaurant openings with Adrift by David Myers, Long Chim by David Thompson, Bread Street Kitchen by Gordon Ramsay, and Spago by Wolfgang Puck, and my son's favourite restaurant, Mozza. We went to Mozza on every special occasion, the staff knew us and made us feel like royalty. How sad that they closed in 2019 because of a sex scandal involving the chefs and partner Mario Batali. By this time, the #metoo Movement was well established, and there was no getting away with bad behaviour. In fact, when Covid-19 came around, MBS restaurants would make up a fair share of the casualties, and many of them would eventually close their doors too.

The opening of MBS lifted the culinary standards for Singapore, but it also changed the playing field for staff and recruiting local talent. Since money was no object for the owner of MBS, Sheldon Adelson, they were able to pay higher salaries than other hotels and free standing restaurants. After all, this was a casino, even though they called it an integrated resort, and their profits were incomparable to other businesses.

For Wild Honey, since the opening of the Mandarin Gallery outlet, business was still peaking and we considered expanding into units 03–01 and 03–03, but both were occupied. People would stop me on the street and tell me that my problem was that Wild Honey was too popular. A good problem to have, but now the question of when the right time is to expand confronted us. By 2010, Stephanie had happily resigned her position with JWT and was focusing on helping Alex with school. She was in charge of all marketing communication, creative direction, and menu design. It was a huge help for me as this was truly her forte. Stephanie and I had just returned from a vacation in northern Italy where we ate in the most incredible restaurants. Impressions of Rome and Tuscany were fresh in our minds, as was the issue of expansion.

Orchard Road was still our first choice as it was retail central. During this time, we were invited by Wheelock Properties to view a presentation at their headquarters by Bee Q, their general manager. They informed us that they were going to reopen the old Scotts Square Mall, which was where the first food court had opened in Singapore twenty years ago. The project was very impressive, with a luxury residential tower above the mall. In fact, when we used to drive home from work, Steph would point at the construction project—in particular the third floor balcony—and say it would be a great place for Wild Honey. The opening of the tower was planned for November 2011 and they had one exclusive unit 03–01 and 02, which would have a veranda with outdoor seating overlooking Scotts and Orchard Road. The unit was huge, 3,300 square feet, compared to our first outlet. They invited us for a site inspection, and Stephanie liked the unit immediately. I felt that we were not ready for such a big step and was afraid of the size of the project. Still, we needed to expand and at some point, I gave in, and we signed a three-year agreement. We now had six months to prepare. Here we go once again!

* * *

First, we needed a designer and we found Mathew Shang, who ran a boutique agency with quality work. They had won some prestigious awards for their designs, which included the Manhattan Bar, The Hour Glass, and The Club Hotel Singapore, to name a few. The feel of the restaurant in Mandarin Gallery was of a New York loft with dark fabrics and red bricks. This new project was going to be more Californian with brighter colours, outdoor seating, more plants and decorations, and a shopfront that would resemble a Florentine bakery or candy shop. Stephanie, once again, took over the creative leadership of the project. The concept this time was to bring elements of rural domestic life combined with city savvy to an all-day breakfast restaurant. It was a new concept, but what would remain was that it was again designed to bring the feeling of 'home' to those travelling or seeking comforting food. Its varied table settings, the informal backdoor style entrance, and the outdoor veranda were brought to life by an eclectic palette of materials and objects inspired by bountiful Australian homesteads and casual spaces from around the globe. The entrance was to replicate the casual feeling of passing through a kitchen in order to reach the more formal living room. Colourful, custom-designed floor tiles were manufactured in Bali, and it had a hint of Marrakech with a Moorish feel. Beaded curtains filtered the sun through the windows reinforcing the relaxed indoor-outdoor atmosphere. Vibrant textiles presented a cacophony of colours and patterns from bold stripes to tropical forest. This was to become our new shop at Scotts Square.

Then, we needed to find a solid and experienced executive chef to hire, train, and lead the new culinary team. I had no human resources manager at that time, and I did not even have an office. So, all my meetings happened in our dining room. I was working with a recruiter called Michelle Ong, but she was better at recruiting front-of-house staff than those with culinary expertise. So, once again, I approached Andreas and, this time, made him an offer he could not refuse. He accepted and resigned his position as chief culinary instructor in Sun Rice institute. Andreas had helped with the Mandarin Gallery kitchen, but this time round, we had much more space. There was a bar area, and the kitchen would include luxuries like a walk-in chiller, a receiving and prep area, a pastry station, a hot line including American range stove tops and ovens with a griddle, grill, salamander, and a white board to write messages. 'Clean as you go' is a Wild Honey standard message.

The menu was also going to be expanded to include salads and sandwiches and more cakes and desserts. What was new was that this time, the service style would be a full sit-down service with printed menus, which meant it would lose that intimacy of people ordering at the counter. Another change would be the napkins. In the first shop, we used cotton napkins and had them washed by a laundry service, but for the new restaurant, Stephanie designed new paper napkins with beautiful floral designs that would decorate the tabletops, an artistic touch to make our guests feel the brand experience.

We had different challenges with this outlet. One of the windows faced CINQ hair salon, which was directly opposite the unit, so we needed to find a creative way to block the view without losing the natural light. Another challenge was the four-metre-high ceiling. The design team presented us with different solutions on mood boards and material boards. The shop would have outdoor seating with a lounge feeling, like being in a beach club in Ibiza or Phuket. Electric shutters would operate via remote control. Every single piece of furniture was designed by Stephanie and the furniture-maker from Bali. She flew back and forth to the factory in Bali to check on the details of the work. We went back to the same main contractor, Quen Mei, in the capable hands of Steven Lew. Our budget was SG $1 million, but we ended up spending $1.3 million. It would have been worse if I had not cut many design elements and simplified them. For example, the designers wanted electric sliding doors for the outside area. Cut. They wanted special signage for the outside. Cut. This design firm was not good at cost control, and this created a stressful atmosphere and became a real pressure point for the entire team.

Andreas was the same. He wanted the best of everything in the new kitchen with no regard to cost control. Cut, cut, and cut. I began to resent some of the changes and felt threatened and territorial, especially because Stephanie was more involved and possessed many skills that I did not have. The dynamic became competitive and added stress to both of us.

A new outlet also meant new challenges for staffing. The recruitment for service and culinary staff was very weak because of restrictions on foreign workers by the Ministry of Manpower. Culturally speaking, Singaporeans do not like to work in the service industry, and the food and beverage field has a very bad reputation for long hours, late nights, drunk guests, and low pay at $10 an hour. Recruiting Singaporeans was difficult because of the prejudices against the industry, and there were very few role models for young Singaporeans to copy. The industry just lacks 'sex appeal'. At the new outlet, because of the seating size of one hundred and ten, the service crew was more important. In addition to the guest relations officer and the manager on duty, we would need four captains or butlers, one drinks runner, eleven food runners, six baristas, and ten part-time servers and bussers.

The situation in the kitchen was even more dire. As head chef, Andreas needed a second-in-command and two prep cooks, two line cooks, four chef de parties, and a pastry chef. Stewarding would be outsourced like the first outlet. Recruitment was very slow and draining. We were just not able to attract talent, and they were put off knowing how busy the first restaurant was. Time was running out, and the pressure was on. Having no choice, we hired green culinary graduates from Sunrise to fill the positions. They were not ready for any opening and especially not the volumes we saw at Wild Honey. In the end, the problem was that we were unprepared for the expansion into Scotts. The team was not strong enough to service the giant dining area of 120 seats. The worst thing was that I knew this. The gut-wrenching trepidation that I had going into opening day, having already been terrified that the whole endeavour was too large for us, was like the hollow banging of a death knell.

* * *

The result on opening day, 11 November 2011, was that my worst fears were realized—massive food delays and many unhappy guests. Andreas and his team could not keep up, and we made the mistake of not reducing the menu to allow the team to practice more of the same dishes. The disaster was complete when some of the newly graduated students from Sunrise (these were Andreas' students, no less) walked out. I handled it very badly by causing a confrontation that almost became physical, and the disaster was taken to the next level when this somehow led to us being raided by the Ministry of Manpower.

In the USA, you fear the FBI. In Singapore, with low to almost no crime rate, the Ministry of Manpower is the feared authority for the service industry. They entered the restaurant at Scotts Square, no guns drawn, but with body cams and the police in tow. It was incomprehensible: it was just two weeks after opening, and we were in full service. They started to interrogate my staff with no consideration for the dining guests, and I once again handled the situation very badly. Confronting and being aggressive with government officials was unproductive, but the problem was that I was highly emotional. In layman's terms, I was having a meltdown. I could not understand how Wild Honey had suddenly appeared on their radar, and it was only later that I put the pieces together that the students had probably made a complaint. I was horrified and very, very embarrassed to be under investigation. They claimed that I was employing illegal workers, which was simply not true. They took pictures of the team like we were criminals. The investigating officer was a young lady, and she accused me of back paying and under declaring the salaries of foreign workers. This also was not true.

Meanwhile, the MoM investigation continued. It was like they wanted to make Wild Honey the poster child of offenders against the employment act. A few days passed, and I received a letter in the mail from the investigating officer, informing me that I might be deported from Singapore and that I should inform the US embassy of this possibility. Wow, this was a new low. My business was here, my life was here, and my son was at school happily settled. It felt like I had been found guilty without a hearing. I was devastated and completely demotivated to continue my work. Stephanie and I brainstormed and approached Drew & Napier, a prestigious law firm, who wrote a strong reply to the ministry, challenging their findings. A few weeks later, I was invited for my first labour court case. The charge was underpaying hourly wages, and, in the end, the charges were dropped. What a waste of time and resources! These events left me feeling wounded, and my respect for the great city state shaken.

The rules for hiring foreign workers in Singapore are very complex. Our financial controller, whom we relied on to give us the right advice, strongly recommended that we create a separate company for the new business, principally considering that every new restaurant is high risk. He pointed out the financial advantages of having a separate company, like not paying the Goods and Services Tax for the first SG $1 million revenue. It made sense to us at the time, but what he did not explain was that by separating both companies, we would not be able to transfer labour from our first company, and even worse, we would have no quota to hire foreign workers. This turned out to be a major mistake. Looking back, we should have opened the second restaurant under the same company because labour is actually the biggest issue in the restaurant business in Singapore. This caused us grave issues going forward. The financial controller failed to think holistically about our business needs. Rather than just following the textbook, he should have looked at *our* needs in particular. This lack of lateral thinking and, let us face it, just using common sense impacted our business and was a trait I came across more than once in Singapore. This left me very sour.

These were the business problems, but, in the meantime, the press once again welcomed us. One month after Scotts Square and Wild Honey Scotts Square opened, *Epicure*, in its December 2011 issue, wrote: 'It is no longer the place to go for a bowl of gravy slathered beef noodles, but a gleaming Scotts Square has sprouted up where Scotts Picnic used to sit, and with it, two dining spots we love. Wild Honey, its second, is more than just a replica of the popular all-day breakfast at Mandarin Gallery. You will immediately notice the veranda that peeks out to Orchard Road, plus you are spared the walk to the counter to place your order—full table service is offered here. You might be tempted to stick to favourites like the Tunisian ($18), but new stunners like the Persian ($24)—caramelized French toast with baked black plums, orange segments, thick homemade labneh, orange blossom and saffron syrup, and the Roman ($22)— an open faced egg frittata crowned with rosemary scented potatoes, white truffle oil, mascarpone and Avruga caviar—are worth ordering too. The real deal clincher: you can now beat the queues by making a reservation, regardless of how small your party is.'

Who does not love a positive review?

Then, like I was in a horrible loop, my second chef quit. Andreas was going through a divorce, and things at Wild Honey were very tense and negative. He was not delivering, and clearly,

I had backed the wrong horse. His departure within twelve months of the new outlet opening again left me unprepared. I noticed a pattern, which was that chefs do not seem to groom their second-in-command. So, when they leave, it is left to the owner to take control over the kitchen, which is difficult without culinary training. Most unfair. Luckily, I mentioned the problem to my yoga instructor from Bangkok, and she had a brother in Singapore working at the St Regis as an executive chef. So, I approached Christian Bruhns, and he became Wild Honey's chef number three. He needed a change, and I offered him the position of head chef at Wild Honey, Scott Square. He readily accepted the position. Christian specialized in Italian food, and his white butter sauce with fresh winter truffle became our truffle benedict special. It was dangerously delicious. He added some important protocols and was more of a leader and mentor for the young culinary team.

Then, out of nowhere, in 2013, in less than six months since he had begun work, my chef number three Christian decided to leave his wife and at the same time resigned from his position. Was I cursed or had I killed a chef in my previous life? Nobody was surviving the Wild Honey kitchen show. I was no Gordon Ramsay but I had to take command of the kitchen now. I would prep in the morning, expedite dishes out during peak hours, order food, and in between prayed for a miracle. My hotel training helped me troubleshoot and stay positive, and by rotating staff from both kitchens, things started to slowly turn around. Luckily, my front-of-house leaders were strong enough to manage many areas while I was acting head of kitchen. Eventually, in 2014, we promoted a young female CDP, Chef number four, to lead that team, and she did a fantastic job until she left for maternity leave. Chef Maan, we miss you.

Expansion, labour raids, and resigning chefs, we were grateful to be surviving.

Chapter 16

Overexpansion

It was 2015, and we had been open for over six years now. With Stephanie on board, we really needed creative outlets. Opening and running a successful restaurant did not inspire us enough and we wanted to explore new ideas. Creativity is key in this business, and we were constantly trying to think out of the box. During a brainstorming session, we came up with a revolutionary idea. What about a midnight brunch? We would partner with Culina, who were the representatives for Chandon Sparkling Wines, and would host a midnight brunch, including free flow wine, a DJ, and a live drummer. The idea was to create a party atmosphere. Our customers loved the idea, and the event was sold out.

A reception was held on the rooftop of Mandarin Gallery to create a dramatic start for the event. We invested in white balloons and a funky lit up bar. Finger food was served, including Brazil breads, mini burgers, mini tarts, smoked salmon, fish roe, and other goodies. Then, after the initial splash upstairs, the guests were moved downstairs to Wild Honey. They were welcomed by a cool vibe. The room was decorated with flowers and buckets of Chandon, and upon entry, flutes of chilled sparkling wine were served. This was new to us and proved that we could also cater small private events for up to fifty people.

This became a tradition for Wild Honey: one-off events to give our customers variety, stimulate our creativity, and just add a bit of joie de vivre all around.

The frightening thing about the restaurant business is how fast restaurants go out of business. I was always anxious and often felt like I was treading water just to make sure we sustained the momentum. Jones the Grocer in Dempsey had opened the same year that we had and was a major success. Their outlet in Mandarin Gallery was our direct competitor located on Level 4, just one floor above Wild Honey. But in 2013, Jones the Grocer Mandarin Gallery closed. The shop had no windows, did not have any atmosphere, and foot traffic was very slow. Then, the owner sold the brand license for SEA. and the Middle East to the LVMH group. It was mismanaged and lost direction because they had no experience in running restaurants. They overexpanded into ION Shopping Mall but could not attract the masses they had at their flagship shop at Dempsey. It was a total disaster, and they closed within a year. I watched and thought I was learning, but little did I know that I was soon to experience the same disaster in a costlier way.

It was 2015, we now had two super popular outlets in Mandarin Gallery and Scotts Square. Each one was different, with some people preferring the original cool gem while others appreciated the more spacious and sophisticated Scotts Square. It was six years since we had opened, and it was time to renew the lease for Mandarin Gallery. We expressed our intention to extend, however the landlord kept us waiting for nine months. I became impatient and, in the meantime, decided to move the small shop at 03–02 into a larger space on the same floor. Then question of whether to combine both units 03–01 and 03–02 came up, and we thought maybe we could use the old space as a private dining room or enlarge the kitchen for the new restaurant. This would have been the prudent thing to do, but Stephanie also wanted to flex her artistic muscles. She was very interested in my Jewish background and came up with an amazing idea; open a New York Jewish style deli in the old Wild Honey space. I loved the idea, and we immediately started research and planning for the new business. This was the beginning of the story of Sacha & Sons.

* * *

Many people ask me why I opened another concept when Wild Honey was already so popular. The answer was that we missed New York and our old home, and this would bring New York a bit closer to Singapore. Wild Honey was all about breakfast, but the concept was limited in its scope. The new deli, Sacha & Sons, would allow us more creative freedom and not place any restrictions on us. Moreover, it would give us the chance to fly back to New York to research all the great delis we remembered from our time living there. Sadly, because of pressure from work, we were unable to leave Singapore that year. That would make our R&D for this new venture more challenging. The process of conceptualizing, creating, and opening Sacha & Sons was a wonderful experience, a project that was very close to our hearts. Stephanie was in charge as project manager and appointed The Stripe Collective to create the branding story and design the interiors. Our budget for the project was very limited, so we did not even renovate the kitchen, which saved some money, and everything that could be recycled from Wild Honey was to be used.

Kelly Dickinson was the owner and creative director of the agency and had a really cool vision. She requested for my family pictures from Eastern Europe and Israel and copied them onto wooden blocks that were used as decorations on the side wall. This gave the shop a retro, old world feel, and being able to see my great grandparents, uncles, and my father as a young boy really made me feel great. My heritage was on the wall, a story for people to see, a little piece of my history here in Singapore. Stephanie created a brand book with all the logos, napkins, plates, stickers, straws, cake boxes, soda bottles, and hand painted sign boards in black and white, displaying 'Sacha & Sons, since 1929'. Other design elements included hand painted signboards, neon lights, and black and white checkered floor tiles. She truly gave it a personality and history that was so unique and original, and as far as I knew, there was nothing like this in Southeast Asia. Again, we were breaking new ground, forging ahead, taking a risk.

We loved deli fare. The ingredients for the Jewish deli fare would be critical. A central element in the menu would be good beef brisket pastrami from the USA. This cut was not available in Australia, so we used Angus US, and Stephanie worked with our meat supplier, experimenting with different recipes and settled on a dry cure instead of a wet cure. The cure had salt, coriander, garlic, and paprika. After two weeks of marinating, the meat would be steamed for four hours and then smoked in wooden chips for another four hours.

My challenge was to design a cutting board and steamer that would house the meat once it arrived vacuum-packed from our butcher. The cutting would be done in the front as a showpiece for people to see and smell the meat. This was a deli tradition in New York and Montreal: to see the cutter in action. This was the way it was done in places like Katz's Deli, Carnegie Deli, and Zabars. The board would be a heavy butcher's block inserted into a steel envelope that allowed the board to slide in and out. Another feature was to catch the debris from the board onto a side lip that protruded out. The steamer on wheels was placed directly underneath, and this allowed the deli man to take the still-hot meat out and place it on the cutting board to do his ceremonial cutting. It was hard work and a true labour of love. In fact, one of the reasons many delis in the US went out of business was because it was such backbreaking work and the children of the owners did not want to take over and work that hard.

Of course, the other major challenge would be producing the perfect bagel because we had never made them before. Stephanie worked together with our pastry head, and after many trials they decided to use the Montreal method. The process starts with making the dough and then portioning it to 120 gm. This rests at room temperature for twenty minutes to proof, then a hole is made in the centre like a doughnut, proof again for twenty minutes, add honey into boiling water, and then poach the bagels for one to two minutes on each side. Finally, coat with sesame seeds and bake for twenty-three minutes at 160°C. A very intensive labour of love and our team positively hated making them. This was a setback for us but, nevertheless, we baked fresh bagels seven days a week from 5 a.m. to 8 a.m. Stephanie designed attractive wooden towers to display our new treasures which people could have with strawberry jam, plain cream cheese, salmon cream cheese, trout salad, egg salad, and the all-time crowd favourite, jalapenos chili cream cheese. Endless possibilities with our bagels.

Who doesn't like bagels? The mixing and matching— *mishung* in Yiddish—deli was fun! Or so we thought, but our local customers did not like bagels! Unfortunately, many locals had never travelled to old New York, and they confused deli with diner, requesting hotdogs and hamburgers. They confused pastrami with salami and could not understand what all the fuss was about. Another lesson for us was that beef was not a staple in Singapore because many Buddhists did not eat beef. We also had many requests for pork, which we declined for the sake of authenticity and tradition. Sincerity in food is critical.

Another problem was that the price point was high because all the ingredients needed had to be imported and created from scratch. One kilogram of sturgeon fish from France was SG $150, and a kilo of beef brisket was SG $30; so, making a profit on this menu was challenging.

* * *

When Sacha & Sons opened in 2015, I was immensely proud of our offering. We had old sugar glass jars from New York City, special uniforms, chicken schnitzel, smoked trout salad, chopped liver, hand rolled bagels, cheese blintzes, egg and onion salad, potato salad, flavoured cream cheese, grilled pastrami Reuben, corned beef, roast beef, classic chicken soup with maze balls, New York cheesecake, cherry and apple strudel, milkshakes, and handmade sodas. Eventually, we even made our own mustards. Some other highlights on the menu included homemade sour pickles, which took a lot of experimenting with vinegar, salt, garlic, and dill. It was especially frustrating because we could not find the ideal vertical cucumber. We also made latke, which are potato fritters that go well with applesauce and sour cream, and, of course, everything goes well with smoked salmon, onion, and fish roe.

Singapore has a vibrant Jewish community that originated from Iraq and became traders and money changers until they settled in the outpost of Singapore some 200 years ago. The community in Singapore is very traditional and sadly was not open to embracing Sacha & Sons because we decided not to get kosher certification. This would have entailed being closed on the Sabbath and would have meant struggling from a business perspective. It was a real shame. I thought we would at least have our Jewish market. Still Sacha & Sons was able to produce first class deli fare and we were awarded 'Best Pastrami' by a local magazine. I have never regretted opening Sacha & Sons because the venture had meant so much for me from a cultural perspective. The reception by those that knew New York deli fare was so heartening. Ronen Arielly, a Jewish resident of Singapore, commented after eating there, 'This is the most full-flavoured, incredible beef-brisket pastrami. A lovely taste of pepper and salt. It's soft and moist, melts in the mouth, with nice lines of fat, and has a nice texture.' Our Reuben was commented on by Daniel Ang in his online food diary: 'The pastrami woo-laa-laa made me salivate with joy for the moment. So good. Tender, juicy, amazingly smoked, perfectly flavoured, appeared in a drool worthy pink hue.' Many of the reviews compared us to the iconic Katz's Delicatessen from New York, and just to be mentioned with that famous deli, which opened all the way back in 1888, was an achievement for me.

I look at everything as part of the learning curve, and the silver lining was that Sacha & Sons led to more innovation in delivery. Wild Honey did not have the trajectory to do delivery, but Stephanie thought that deli fare would travel well and worked tirelessly to enlist the services of Deliveroo. Deliveroo was a new start-up from London created by William Shu, who was inspired by the lack of food delivery availability in the area he worked in. Sacha & Sons became one of their first accounts in Singapore. However, I did really resent paying a 30 per cent commission for the service in an industry, which only makes a 10 per cent profit. We had no choice though because foot traffic was slow on Level 3, and we were competing against ... guess who? Yes—Wild Honey next door. We thought having both brands back-to-back would complement each other, but people were so loyal to Wild Honey, they just walked right by Sacha & Sons. The spill over effect we were banking on just did not materialize, so we needed to create a new client base from scratch. A very tall order indeed but the idea was that delivery would help to get the brand on wheels and very visible. The attractive packaging also helped give a real punch to the product. Soon, deliveries accounted for 30 per cent of the deli's business. Later, Uber food, Odell and Food Panda would jump on the bandwagon. I would not fully appreciate the strength of delivery until five years later, during Covid-19, when it would become 100 per cent of our sales.

Sadly, from a commercial perspective, the deli was only breaking even, so, we decided to sell it. We broke even, but the feeling of giving up was very sad for us both. Stephanie's devotion and sacrifice would never really be appreciated.

I now found myself increasingly frustrated. Ask any husband-and-wife business team and the recurrent issue will always be that you go to work, and you discuss work; you go home, and the work goes with you. All the problems are with you both 24/7, and Stephanie and I did not agree on many things. They may not have been major differences but we had no escape. The Sacha & Sons joint venture had caused some real problems for me. Despite my joy at creating the New York deli concept as it truly reflected my culture, the project had stretched me thin. I had neglected the two original restaurants, and I increasingly blamed Stephanie for mooting the idea in the first place. The deli was more her baby than mine, and I began to feel a loss of control over my business. In other words, I stupidly got territorial. I wanted a new project. I wanted to flex my muscles and have something that was mine, that I could escape to. That nagging feeling was always there with me that I needed to prove myself. It was absurd given that Wild Honey was doing well, but that feeling persisted. Stephanie had encouraged me to open the restaurant, she had supported me, and her direction at critical moments had been fundamental to our success. However, in some ways, perhaps not very maturely, I resented it. I wanted to break out and do something of my own. A man marking his territory. Perhaps not the soundest motivation to expand a business.

In 2015, we were approached by Pavilion Kuala Lumpur to open a Wild Honey in their mall. Around the same time, our coffee supplier, Common Man Coffee Roasters, were in the process of opening a cafe and coffee academy in Malaysia, so the timing seemed right for an overseas expansion there. In hindsight my experiences in Kuala Lumpur were probably based on not doing the groundwork and understanding just how different things were across the causeway. Although Malaysia is a stone's throw from Singapore, it was a completely different environment. I paid a heavy price for that mistake.

* * *

From the get-go, the project was fraught. We travelled to Kuala Lumpur and viewed a ground floor unit, but it occupied an odd shape; not good Feng Shui. We decided to take a much larger unit on Level 5. I tried to purchase the existing Italian restaurant in its current condition before they tore it back to its bare, which would have saved us up to SG $500,000. However, the owners refused, and so we needed to build it from scratch. Once we signed the three-year lease agreement, we started construction in October with the goal of opening in December 2015. Construction was very slow as we were not approved to work during the day. The general working pace was slower and less efficient than in Singapore. The space combined two units together totalling 3,500 square feet, including an outside area. The local designer we hired had to deal with the challenges of very high ceilings, which impacted air flow. Part of the ceiling was open, which meant that noise would flow inside from the public areas.

Apart from the design issues, we had so many problems with creating the business entity. I believed that our chief financial officer in Singapore would be able to create the business entity in Malaysia and register the company for GST. However, he was not familiar with the taxation laws and did not travel to Kuala Lumpur as we had agreed. The supervision of cashflow was very poor, and because we started construction in October but did not register the company until December, all our tax invoices which paid for GST were not recognized as expenses. This mistake alone cost us SG $50,000. Unfortunately, we never got the money back even though the GST was cancelled in 2018. It was an ominous start.

A supportive landlord, as we had learnt in Singapore, is crucial to success, and we stumbled here as well. Negotiations with the landlord proved to be difficult, and the signals were not positive. They had invited us to Kuala Lumpur and planned on opening the new pavilion within twenty-four months, so we thought they would be very much behind us. However, they were focused on their other developments and things seemed to go from bad to worse.

We thought that having a trusted and known partner in Kuala Lumpur would make sense, so we decided to promote our head chef, Chuan Thomas, to a partner and make him the project manager for Kuala Lumpur. Chef Thomas had been with us as second-in-command under Chef Jimmy and was loyal and hardworking. He was a great asset in the kitchen, and we called him Cool hand Luke because he was extremely fast on the hotline and would not get confused during a busy service period when more than 10–15 tables shot out of the printer. Cool hand Luke Chuan was never rattled by pressure. He grew and developed with me over many years and even met his wife Roselle at Wild Honey.

Those sorts of connections always felt significant to me. He was also from Kuala Lumpur and was going to have a baby, so this all made sense as it would also mean he would be near his family. He did not need to invest his own money, and we put the company under Stephanie's and his name.

We hired a local general manager called Tony, based on a personal recommendation from Chef Barry Iddles from Melbourne. Tony was invited to Singapore for an induction into Wild Honey, and he arrived young and enthusiastic about leading the team. In addition, with two restaurants in Singapore and one opening in Kuala Lumpur, we decided to hire a corporate chef from Australia, Chef Tim. Tony arrived in October, and his brief was to oversee all kitchens and assist Chef Thomas with the opening of the new venture. Chef Tim as group chef was responsible for all three shops and was supposed to oversee and support the Kuala Lumpur team. This arrangement did not prove productive. Chef Tim was travelling with me every week, but he was not hands-on and did not gel with the Kuala Lumpur team. To make matters worse, he did not see eye-to-eye with Tony, and this created tension and conflict between the team. He was unable to control food costs in Kuala Lumpur, and since the delivery rate by suppliers was 50 per cent, we took heavy losses. Exacerbating the situation was the fact that some suppliers were not honest, again a stark contrast to Singapore. In Singapore, your word is your 'word'.

Despite the setbacks, we seemed ready to go, but my intuition was telling me that this project was in deep trouble. So many things were wrong. Clearly, I had chosen the wrong people, we had gone down-market instead of upmarket to Japan or Thailand, the location was wrong, and we had no foot traffic on Level 5. In addition, our construction costs had shot over budget to SG $1 million because inspections and building approvals were not passed without 'contributions.' The exchange rate was three times higher than in Singapore because of the weaker Malaysian currency. Many suppliers underdelivered and tried to substitute quality brands with cheap replacements. When our coffee was shipped from Singapore, it would get stuck in customs and they would demand a 'contribution' for their staff party, and work permits would not be approved unless a runner was paid off. Then, to top it all off, the landlord did nothing to promote the opening of Wild Honey.

Was this place the next Singapore, we asked ourselves? Clearly, it was not. I had worked in five countries and had never seen anything like the working environment in Malaysia. The sales from that December were MR 600,000, but our guests were not happy with their experience. The menu was not well received, and the prices proved too high for locals. One day, when I was away on a trip to Australia, Tony resigned. This was a massive blow. I started to rotate my managers from Singapore to Kuala Lumpur, but they hated the travel. The female managers did not feel very safe in such a big city, and the men did not like the travel. The constant travelling also started to affect my health and wellbeing, I was not enjoying the experience and started to become resentful towards the project. I had made a mistake. I had expanded for the wrong reasons. I had become overconfident and forgotten that what had made me a success was that I had my trusted partner Stephanie at my side. I had allowed the strain on our marriage to blur my business instincts, and it had led to the wrong decision. Like a car crashing in slow motion, I watched each setback, knowing deep inside that this was going to end in disaster, but I was too far down the road to do anything.

The kicker came when our chef and partner Thomas resigned after less than one year. His wife Roselle resented the move to Kuala Lumpur and increasingly disrupted her husband's work. A chef's resignation had become a Wild Honey staple, but this was a wholly different problem because he was our local partner for legal reasons, which left us in a difficult position. In the kitchen, there was no second-in-command trained to take over, but most of all, Thomas leaving broke what little spirit I had left. After a year of disappointments and flat growth, we decided to sell the business. We found a buyer who purchased the restaurant in an 'as is' condition and took a franchise for the territory of Malaysia. The franchise was sold for US $300,000, and this helped offset the massive loss for us.

* * *

I took solace in the positive developments in Singapore. During this period, we moved Wild Honey Mandarin Gallery into its new location. This time, we collaborated with Antonio from We Craft Design Group. He was a pioneer of soulfully designed architecture and design thinking. From the moment we met Antonio Eraso, the co-founder and chief design officer, we felt a strong connection. He totally understood the brand and how personal it was for us. Having designed the Jing and Pollen Restaurants in Phuket, Antonio came with the highest pedigree. The corner unit 03–01 was an art gallery called MAD before we took over, and we wanted to somehow keep that vibe in the new design. We worked with a super talented artist, Melanie Walker, who began her artistic journey on the island of Barbados. She relies on her innate sensibilities, using a combination of memory, observation, and emotion to create her work. As a fan of Wild Honey, she was receptive to the idea of a creative collaboration. The theme for the new Wild Honey at Mandarin Gallery was New York City, so she created a magical skyline. The painting was so heavy, we needed four workers to hang the two giant panels she painted. We love the piece, and many people stop and snap a picture of themselves in front of her work.

For the shop's design, the idea was to take some elements from the old shop like NY grunge and loft into the new space.

The windows were decorated with steel frames to give it an industrial feel. We were now playing with 3,300 square feet in unit 03–02, so we added a guest bar with fourteen seats and displayed the pastry area, so people would see our beautiful handmade creations. We also created a waiting area with a daybed in the entrance. We needed to give the space intimacy and familiarity because our regulars would need to accept this new Wild Honey.

In the meantime, our chef woes continued. Around this time, we realized that Chef Tim was not the head chef we were looking for, so we agreed to part ways. Before hiring him, we failed to do our due diligence and check his background. Although Tim had said he was a senior head chef, his skills did not demonstrate this. Reputation is everything in life and those who do not do background checks end up overpaying and disappointed. An expensive mistake on my part as importing him from Melbourne had been costly. Exit chef number five. After that, it has been a revolving door of chefs: William, Mann, Thomas, now Joseph. I have lost count, but I live in the hope that Wild Honey can keep a chef.

Still, our two outlets in Singapore were doing well, and I am nothing if not eternally optimistic.

Chapter 17

Delegate

Labour problems.

Ask any restaurateur in Singapore what their biggest challenge is, and they will all say the same thing. Labour. From the start, I had been interviewing, screening, hiring, on-boarding, and training most of the employees on my own. The labour laws in Singapore were constantly being updated, and this made me feel anxious and unprepared. Not having a human resources office for several years made us more focused on the priorities of taking care of our guests, but by 2015, we had grown to a staff of fifty. I had handled the HR throughout the opening of new outlets, expansions, renovations, and moves.

I had learned lessons the hard way. Back when business was driven by a lot of cash transactions, we would deposit them daily, except on weekends and holidays. This meant sometimes we had a large amount of cash in our safe overnight. An MOD of ours 'borrowed' $25,000 from our safe to bet on the outcome of a sports match. When I discovered the missing money, he tried to run away to Malaysia, but the police caught him, and he served seven months in prison. We never got the money back, but for me it was not the money, it was the betrayal. This employee had worked for us for three years, and we trusted him.

We felt sick to our stomach to think that someone working for us was capable of stealing.

I also handled service recovery, and although every restaurateur will have a story or two to tell on this, nothing quite beats our baby Jane story. It took me years to be able to talk about it because it was so horrific. One night, an Indonesian family with their young baby was having dinner, and our closing team was restless and wanted to start closing procedures. One of the servers (who I have to admit I instinctively did not like) carelessly and vindictively wrote on the order 'baby must die'. This accidentally got attached to the captain's order on the guest's check for payment. The poor parents went from saddened to enraged pretty rapidly. In the end, building security was called in and had to make an official report. The next morning, when Stephanie and I read the manager's log, we nearly had a heart attack. Without any hesitation, I fired the part-time staff involved. Unfortunately, this resulted in a massive walk out of all the part-time staff in solidarity, which would result in heavy losses as we faced a severe staff shortage. The staffs' loyalty was to each other, not to us, their employer. It was a crushing disappointment to us, and, at the same time, we had to go into crisis management mode.

I hope we faced the situation with respect and graciousness. We went to Takashimaya and purchased a wooden gift basket, filled it with champagne, chocolates, stuffed animals, cheeses, bread, and just whatever goodies we could find, attached a letter apologizing profusely for the shocking incident and invited them back with gift vouchers. I got their address from the security report and hand delivered it to their doorstep. When I rang the doorbell, I was terrified, and my heart was going through the roof. They did not open the door to me. I was met with dead silence. I left it at their doorstep, and two days later, we received an email from them thanking us for caring and reaching out. They never did come back.

I had handled HR for too long, and I was exhausted. I wanted to be on the creative side, create events, look for new opportunities, perhaps even expand again. I did not want to keep handling staff issues because, being so emotionally invested in the company, I was not objective or productive. We needed to create a new HR position, but the problem was that HR was ten years behind the US in terms of understanding, communication, delegation, motivation, and leadership. Horror stories of local restaurateur friends and my own interviews with prospective applicants made it apparent that a good number of local HR managers seemed to lack creativity and problem-solving skills. Both of these attributes are imperative in the service industry in Singapore because of the high turnover of labour. In addition, they were notably not specialized in F&B retail. Adding to this, restaurants in Singapore rely heavily on staff from the region, and I was on a constant merry-go-round of endless applications for work passes, training, staff quitting, and starting the process again and again.

Now, I went into a spate of hiring to try and find the right person to handle the HR issues. First was Sunny, who became my personal assistant to take over this aspect of management. Sunny turned out to be a huge gossip who enjoyed taking long smoke breaks and did not have the strategic thinking needed for this role. She left after only six months. Then, I hired a South African psychology major who I thought would be able to manage HR because of her human relations skills. People relations skills were all well and good, but her experience in details was lacking and caused me yet again to end up in labour court. One of my employees had come to us with a pre-existing issue with a disability of his hand, which my HR manager neglected to document. He decided to take us to court, claiming this condition was a result of juicing oranges and demanding work men's compensation. You have to hand it to him for creative scamming. Because she had not done her due diligence and documented his disability, the court made our insurance company settle the matter with him. In the end, her relationship with her husband deteriorated and then she suddenly packed up and left for Sydney. Ironically, for an HR manager, she neglected to bother giving me any notice. Interviews for HR managers increased, but nothing interesting came up. In the meantime, I was using recruitment agencies to find staff.

I completely understood the ministry's role in protecting employees, but I could not understand why Wild Honey always seemed to be at the centre of controversy. For instance, when Chef William was unhappy, what better way to go than report us to the ministry? Outright quitting would have been much too easy. His parting gift was to accuse us of hiring illegal people to the Ministry of Manpower and mentioned Jesse's name to them. Jesse, the Filipino who had come to us via the recruitment agency. Jesse, who lives with his wife in Singapore. Jesse, the most hard-working, dedicated employee we had. The ministry could not find any evidence of illegal employees— because we did not hire any—but poor Jesse was part of the fallout of William's accusations. The ministry made a charge against us that Jesse's educational certifications were fake, which meant his employment, under Singapore law, was illegal. This was the one that came back to bite me. I had done my due diligence as an employer, but sadly, Jesse's certificates were fake because the recruitment agency had not checked. When Jesse heard about the investigation, he fled back to the Philippines, leaving his wife in Singapore. To this day, I fail to understand why service staff need to have educational certificates. It seems to me that for the service industry, loyalty, hard work, and a smile are the most important qualifications. Poor Jesse, he was such a wonderful worker and always responsible. So, exit one chef and one valuable employee under the cloud of yet another ministry investigation.

* * *

Why do you remember pain more than pleasure? Investigations from the ministry are excruciating. You are summoned for endless interviews, you carry reams of payroll, bank, and Central Provident Fund (CPF) statements, and it usually ends in nothing. You are interrogated, not just once but over and over. I have been mugshot and threatened with deportation. The stream of court cases—five in total, the frequent investigations—close to ten, this is all part of running a restaurant in Singapore. I try to shut it out of my mind but cannot. It seemed like every time I had a disgruntled employee, they would decide the easiest way to get revenge was to use the labour court. Some of these would be the result of disputes over less than $100. I would be summoned to court and would have to make resolution with the plaintiff and present that to the judge to get the case dismissed. Sometimes, it was a simple matter of them not keeping track of their hours, and off they would run to labour court to dispute their pay. Other times, they used the labour court as a way of getting back at me for something unconnected. Like I said, I understood the role of the ministry in helping the underdogs from unscrupulous employers, and there are many, but I often felt like my employees used the ministry to subdue me. Look at me the wrong way, and I have this power over you. For this amount of stress, I should have been a famous gangster bringing in the big bucks! In truth, it was all exhausting and demoralizing.

It was actually due to one of these cases that I met the man who would become my new HR manager and advisor, Eddie Tan. It happened when I faced yet another unpleasant labour issue. Cornerstone Recruitment had sent me RT, whom I employed as a restaurant service quality manager. I learned later that he was quite a troubled individual who apparently came from a very wealthy family in Singapore and whose father owned some restaurants in Hong Kong. I think he liked working at Wild Honey but not so much working with me. It came to light that there was some socializing and some dating between him and my younger staff, some of them underage, and it troubled us. When I confronted him, he became aggressive and told me that whatever he did outside of work was his business. He had only been with us six months, and I had such an uncomfortable feeling about the whole thing that I made the decision to let him go. This exploded in my face. He verbally attacked me saying some awful things including threatening my business and telling me he would ensure it suffered. This resulted in a third investigation by the Ministry of Manpower. RT claimed we underpaid our part-time staff. Nothing could be further from the truth because, in fact, we overpay our staff. The investigators spent hours looking through our payroll and bank statements. They found nothing. It was a colossal waste of time and energy.

This is why I went back to Cornerstone to try and get some help with this RT situation. Eddie answered the door of the office. I had never met him as he was not the original recruiter, but I was so upset, I sat down with him and told him the whole story. Eddie had no idea who I was or who RT was, but he was super friendly and supportive and volunteered to go and represent me in labour court and fight for us. It was over and above what I expected or what the agency was obliged to do for me. In the end, RT accepted a pair of new sneakers as compensation, and it never went to court. He had demanded six months' pay instead of accepting the usual four weeks' notice and claimed that his clothes had been damaged at work, which was absurd. He was so angry after his disappointment at arbitration that he went to the Ministry of Labour and claimed that we had not paid him and were not paying our part-timers fairly. Once again, they came in and did a huge investigation but found nothing. The silver lining was that I was so impressed with Eddie realizing that if this person was willing to do something like this for me without asking for anything back, he had real integrity and commitment. I offered him a job. He was really surprised by my offer, but it was one that he could not refuse (I made sure of that), and that is how I finally employed an HR manager.

This was a turning point because Eddie gave me a foundation and a better understanding of working with Singaporeans. Together, we created an HR office from scratch, and he has been with me for four years now. He has been very helpful and supportive of the company, and I am not really sure how I managed without him. Together, we restructured the organizational chart to create higher productivity and doubled the training and development of our team. We worked with Sunrice Global Chef Academy to place culinary students into our kitchens. We also visited career fairs and networked actively. By 2017, HR needed an office, so Eddy found a nice one in the Tong building on Orchard Road, where we could train classroom style with a proper meeting room and no disturbances. Prior to this, most of the training had taken place in the restaurants, which of course clashed with operations. Most importantly, I finally had someone to share the burden of staff difficulties with.

My approach to the service industry in Singapore over the last ten years has had to evolve exponentially. When I started, everything was centred around me because I had nobody to trust. That meant HR, finance, purchasing, operations, service, and many other responsibilities fell on my shoulders. As Stephanie became more involved in the business, and because of my fantastic assistant David, and bringing Eddie on board, I began to learn to delegate some responsibilities and trust people because I was good in some areas and terrible in others. One disaster area was reacting to bad reviews because I took everything to heart, which is why I do not handle the social media aspect of the business. Another area was numbers. I was not good at analysing long financial spreadsheets. The previous type of management style was suited for a single American-style restaurant whereby the leader (me) had black shirts (supervisors) who managed the white shirts (staff). This makes communication easy as the hierarchy is flat. This changed as I began to trust and delegate, and it had to change as I expanded.

This, in turn, gave me more time to maintain quality and to work on the creative side of the business.

Chapter 18

Creativity

Bread and butter, eggs and toast; our tried-and-tested all-day breakfast menu is the mainstay of Wild Honey, but I strongly believe that we have stayed current and vibrant because we are open to new ideas and opportunities.

In 2012, shortly after our Scotts Square outlet had opened, we hosted an event around wine, organized by Monopole. The owner of the winery was Sam Neill—a name Jurassic Park fans are probably familiar with—and he wanted to launch his new vintage press wine in Singapore. We created a special menu just for that launch, and these are some of the greatest wines imaginable. This is a very, very small company, utterly obsessed with Pinot Noir and Riesling, and they take great pride in their organics, their quality, their authenticity, and are meticulous about the details and their style. The company has four fully organic vineyards, artfully scattered around Central Otago, which is the southernmost wine region of New Zealand. They were great fun and do not take themselves seriously at all! The seriousness is all left to their very serious wines. That year, Michael Hill, Australia's first Master of Wine and owner of the winery Shaw + Smith, was also introduced to Wild Honey, again through Monopole. All these wines are featured at Wild

Honey, and events like this gave us a chance to exercise our creative muscles and fine tune our quality.

Perhaps the highlight of these one-off events was in 2014 when we got the chance to cook for the world-renowned maestro Zubin Mehta. One of the world's greatest classical music conductors, he was visiting Singapore to conduct the Israeli Philharmonic Orchestra at their Marina Bay Sands event to celebrate Singapore's 50th birthday. In attendance at the event were the Israeli Ambassador Yael Rubinstein and Singapore's Deputy Prime Minster Teo Chee Hean. I had met Yael in Bangkok when she had requested that I help train her staff in table etiquette and banquet service to prepare for hosting a meal for the Thai royal family. So, when she invited Zubin Mehta and the orchestra to Singapore as Israel's 50th birthday present to Singapore, she requested that I get involved. He was being hosted, along with other VIPs at her house, and Wild Honey provided an Israeli-style brunch on official state crockery for twenty guests. The maestro loved his chilli. I remember he reached into his pocket and took out a private stash of it to put on his shakshuka. That made me smile. I felt proud to contribute in a small way to such a momentous occasion, and before the concert began, the orchestra played the Israeli national anthem. Without realizing it, my Israeli heritage and my new home had become one, and it had a profound impact on me emotionally. I teared up.

* * *

Another great opportunity came our way in 2018 when we were introduced to Yossi Elad. Chef Elad was involved in founding, amongst others, The Palamar in London and Balangan in Paris, restaurants that are considered milestones of the Israeli culinary scene. His establishments have received numerous awards and accolades, and we were huge fans. His philosophy was to cook the food people love to eat, and that was also the foundation of Wild Honey. We met on Skype when he was in the process of opening a new restaurant in Frankfurt, and he was impressed with my German language skills. The chemistry between us just flowed, so I asked him if he would be interested in visiting Singapore to be a guest chef at Wild Honey. We were lucky; he had never been to Asia and loved the idea. We began sharing ideas and experiences, and through these exchanges, we established a certain trust in each other. I was determined to make this happen despite the logistical difficulties. When would Yossi be free? How would we source the ingredients? How complex would the menu be? How would we integrate his menu with Wild Honey's? We wanted him to train and instruct our culinary team and be a mentor and big brother to them. Yossi was looking forward to exploring the local markets and experiencing Singapore. This was not a business contract but a gentleman's agreement that things would be balanced between work, exploration, and fun. I was excited!

It was important to us that Chef Elad's food tasted exactly like it did in his restaurants. Stephanie got more involved in the menu selection and R&D. It was clear that getting the food to have pure Jerusalem flavours was going to be a challenge. The quality of the spices—coriander seeds, paprika, turmeric, cardamom, star anise, fennel seeds, cumin seeds, zaatar, sumac, dried limes, mahler, dried rose petals—we needed to source all these spices before Yossi arrived. He would hand-carry some high-end spices on his journey, but the groundwork and sourcing needed to begin much earlier.

This was also an important cultural milestone for the Israeli cultural scene in Singapore, and to commemorate this, we needed to plan some mini events around his visit. There would be a formal reception at the Israeli ambassador's residence catered by our friend Dennis, owner of Blue Kuzina restaurant in Dempsey Hill, and fully sponsored by Wild Honey. A master class with twenty students would be held in a kitchen lab located in OUE downtown. Dinner with the Ministry of Defence would be organized and hosted by the Israel military attaché. Then, there was the event at Wild Honey. We wanted there to be a fantastic atmosphere, so we invited DJ Malcolm X to spin every night on a local turntable, and we recruited our dear friend and artist Hamish Best to create a market setting at the entrance.

Yossi refused to discuss desserts, so Stephanie took matters into her own hands and created some delicious desserts including a new Middle Eastern spiced ice cream flavour— Ras El Hanut, halva infused sababa brownies, and rosewater malabi pudding. New cocktails were created like Desert Rose in addition to Turkish coffee and a spirit called arak, made from liquorice. We arranged for pita and laffa bread to be baked daily by the Pita Factory on Haji Lane. The dishes would include white tahini and green tahini sauce, a spicy green chilli sauce called schug, labneh cheese, baba ghanoush, matbucha, falafel balls, polenta—Jerusalem style, aubergine and feta bourekas, shakshukit, and musakhan. A feast!

Then, we needed a date, and we settled on the second week in November 2018 for the event. Yossi would fly in from Frankfurt. OUE, our landlord, was kind enough to provide him a room above Mandarin Gallery at what was the Mandarin Meritus Orchard (now the Hilton), and this gave us three months to practice and prepare. Rather than impose an unfriendly 'Set Menu' on our guests, we decided to offer flexibility and creative pairing of dishes. Each table would receive complimentary toasted pita bread with an assortment of dips. I was also happy to contribute by walking around the dining room and drinking shots with anyone in the mood, and even in our kitchen, everyone was more relaxed. This special menu would only be available for six nights. Each seating accommodated one hundred and fifty guests and we wanted to have two sets of seating a night. Very quickly, the event sold out. One couple even travelled all the way from Bangkok to attend.

Yossi arrived on a Sunday night, and I picked him up from Changi Airport. We had a quick dinner in the hotel, and he crashed. The next day, he entered Wild Honey kitchen and immediately commanded the respect of every team member. Everyone wanted to learn from him. I was in awe.

For Chef Yossi cooking was in his bones. In his own words:

I wanted to be a cook from an early age because my father before me was passionate about good food. So this was an inherited passion. I used to help him in the kitchen and in those days everything was freshly obtained. I also learned another important thing which was to respect fresh ingredients. We were lucky as we had neighbours with cows so an endless supply of fresh milk, we kept chickens for their eggs and grew our own vegetables. Freshness made all the difference to the quality of the meals.

Another important ingredient is the heart. When I cook I do so with love because I care about the people that I cook for—and they can taste that love in my food.

This is why recipes are secondary to me. They are just inspiration but the food is always the product of the person who is cooking at that moment, and where their imagination has taken them. There is a phrase I love to quote: "Great chefs copy, genius chefs steal!"

When I opened my restaurant Machneyuda in Israel in 2009 with my partner's we became popular very quickly. Within just five years we took our simple fresh ingredients, imaginative recipes based on family traditions and combined that with love, and we opened Palomar in London. Home away from home, a bit like Wild Honey![1]

This was a tour de force hosted at Wild Honey. Collaborations like this enriched our menu, inspired our staff, and most of all, gave our customers a unique and memorable experience. I looked forward to creating many more experiences like this for our customers and team.

* * *

During this period, expansion plans were still very much on my mind. Our successful shops on Orchard Road were in no small part driven by their location. I was always on the lookout for the next big location, and it finally landed in my lap in a most unexpected way. South Beach is one of Singapore's newest developments. The architect Foster & Partners had the immense task of incorporating four art-deco style conservation buildings from the 1930s and the Singapore Armed Forces Non-Commissioned Officers Club, into a modern concept. This, in turn, had to blend in with the iconic buildings and national monuments surrounding it, which included Singapore's famous Raffles Hotel. The result was impressive. South Beach is a blend of modern architecture and light, with spectacular views of the ocean juxtaposed and fronted by the old colonial black and white club house. Water features heavily in the design concept with fountains connecting the different architectural elements. The result is a playful mix of heights and curves, creating an atmosphere of community and abundance. All this is served by 3 MRT Lines via extensive underground walkways that make it

---

[1] Yossi 'Papi' Elad, 'A Life in Kitchens', *The Palomar Cookbook (MITCHELL BEAZLE)* (Mitchell Beazley: 2006).

highly accessible, while, at the same time, allowing it to remain distinctive and physically separated from the skyscrapers that dominate the nearby skyline.

South Beach is our newest outlet, or as I like to call it, our baby. Like some babies, it arrived a little unexpectedly. We had initially seen the location when we were shopping around for another collaboration that fell through. The location somehow stayed within our periphery because, as appreciators of all things fine, we were impressed by South Beach and sensed it may fit into our latest plans. We had been searching the Central Business District area for some time to accommodate a central kitchen location to reach our customers in that part of town. Our locations on Orchard Road were simply too far away to deliver to the office crowd in the business district, and what we envisaged was a central kitchen to expand our takeaway business.

We decided that South Beach could become our central kitchen, so we presented our idea to the landlords. However, the savvy landlords had other ideas. They felt that Wild Honey would help bring the crowds to South Beach, so they requested we included a takeout option for residents and office workers and then also slipped in the fact that some people may want to sit and eat their takeout, so perhaps we could consider some seats. This, of course, was a completely different concept to the one that we had considered and was considerably more ambitious. The negotiations lasted a few months until we compromised and signed a letter of agreement, targeting an opening in August 2019.

B1–19 was located in the garden below in an atrium, and a provision was made to allow us to use the outside area in the garden for seating. It had originally operated as a Japanese ramen shop from Osaka, and when the owners ran out of money, they left all the equipment inside. This suited us well, providing a fantastic opportunity to flip the fully loaded kitchen, including heavy cooking equipment, into a Wild Honey kitchen. Having been gently pressured into changing our concept, we got fully onboard and excited. We decided to make the atmosphere casual by adding swings and some pet friendly items on the menu. We envisaged cyclists who completed their weekend rides from the nearby east coast leisure area arriving at Wild Honey, bicycle, pet, and an appetite in tow. We would create some special dishes for athletes whilst children could play in the water sprinklers. This would altogether be a very different concept from our other locations.

Construction started in July 2019. Again, we used the reliable and consistent Quan Mei as we had in all our projects in Singapore. We found an interior designer that had a playful approach to the project and loved their inspired idea of a mix of art-deco with hints of Miami Beach meets urban Coney Island. They used bright fluorescent colours to capture the mood, and, as in all our other projects, we used a Feng Shui master to survey the area. Feng Shui brings its own challenges, and we had to relocate the massive three-metre-high twin doors to a different direction without rebuilding the shop front, and we had to add water features in the garden for creating wealth.

Unlike our other outlets, the opening of Wild Honey, South Beach was more muted. Stephanie was away, so that meant additional pressure on me. We opened to a lukewarm reception in August 2109 with none of the bang that accompanied the Orchard Road launch. Despite all my experience, I was anxious for South Beach to quickly do well and was hard on myself when it came to mistakes. I miscalculated the area and decided against my better judgment to close on Sundays because South Beach was in the business district. This proved to be a big mistake. Another setback was that the delivery companies, ironically, didn't deliver. This was another expensive set back.

Business was very soft in the beginning as we had to adjust for a different crowd and make many menu changes because the crowd in South Beach wanted more cafe options. We put one of our more reliable staff Cindy in charge of this outlet because she was highly experienced, and we knew her friendly demeanour would put the guests at ease. We had some other tricks up our sleeves. We opened a central reservations office and pushed everyone to come and try our new place, we created an e-voucher campaign with chope.com, and we worked with event managers and became partners with the first pet fair in Singapore. All this attracted hundreds of people to South Beach; so, I guess the landlords were right about us after all. We also made renewed efforts on our original delivery plan and catered private breakfast meetings for Citi Group bankers, delivering right to their offices in Raffles Place.

* * *

Wild Honey, South Beach hardly had time to prove itself before Covid-19 overwhelmed us all. We had to shut down from March 2020 in line with the Singapore government regulations and only reopened in August. After the closures caused by the pandemic, like all other restaurants that somehow managed to survive being closed for so long, we reopened with new strategies to recuperate our losses and ensure success. This time, we stayed open during the weekends and recommended South Beach to our regular Wild Honey guests, building loyalty table by table, with no shortcuts. It helped to remember people's tastes and preferences, where they liked to sit, who their preferred server was, and, of course, their favourite meal. This made people feel special because people wanted to be remembered and recognized. The team at South Beach did a terrific job of building up a new customer base.

In October of 2020, having only been in operation for nine months, South Beach's Wild Honey became profitable for the first time. In November, we paid bonuses to the kitchen team for working so hard, and, for the first time since its opening, we felt proud of our new baby.

But before any of this could happen, we had to survive the months of shutdown that started in March 2020.

Chapter 19

The Unforeseeable

How do you foresee something that is so outside the realm of experience that even nations are unprepared for it? How do you survive a global pandemic in the retail industry?

Wild Honey did survive the Covid-19 pandemic. We were not prepared, but we had a combination of luck (we had made some fortunate decisions over the past years), generous landlords, and massive support from the Singapore government. It was beyond my comprehension how much the Singapore authorities helped the industry and especially remarkable when compared to many other governments around the world.

Singapore has an engineering mindset in dealing with all its problems—pragmatic, functional, and efficient. When the World Health Organization declared a pandemic on 11 March 2020, the wheels were already turning in the relevant agencies here, and, luckily, they had the experience and training accumulated during the SARS outbreak in 2003. On 7 April 2020, Singapore entered a four-week-long 'circuit breaker', which essentially meant a lockdown, in response to the Covid-19 outbreak that had been developing in the last months of 2019. Singapore was to completely shut down for four weeks, and we were given hardly a few days' notice. This would affect schools, entertainment venues, offices, and this would include all restaurants. Either we went online and focused on delivery, or we shut our shop to see if we could ride out the closure. The initial period was four weeks, but, truthfully, none of us knew where this was heading, and sure enough, on 21 April, the Prime Minister announced that the closure would be extended for another month.

* * *

We closed Scotts Square and our newly opened South Beach outlet. We also took the bold decision to provide twenty-four-hour delivery service and make it island wide. Normally, our provider Deliveroo only had the trajectory for deliveries within a 2.5 km radius from our location, but by partnering with Lalamove, we were able to work much further afield. In addition, in our efforts to support the healthcare industry and show our appreciation, we discounted all first responders with a 50 per cent discount and created a new economy menu.

We also had to very quickly innovate with a new menu. We came up with a market menu, dinner menu, a pantry menu, a stay-at-home menu, and a pairing menu. The market menu included fruits and vegetables, breads, pies, smoked meats, coffee beans, and different kinds of milk. Supermarkets became crowded as wet markets and small shops started to close down. Toilet paper became the new gold standard.

We at Wild Honey were working around the clock to supply our food to our fans all over the island. We set up teams to divide the work with two MODs manning the landlines, and we created a WhatsApp channel for orders. We assigned another two teams to pack the delivery and, thanks to Oddle, we were able to manage the backend by adding new menus daily. Unlike the Gulf War in 1991 or the attacks in New York on 9/11, I knew this war was going to be longer and more deadly. The irony of Covid-19 starting in a food market was not lost on me. By 18 April, McDonald's closed all operations; by April 22nd all Starbucks and all juice shops closed down. It was terrifying to watch. The chains that were able to reorganize centralized their production and output to one location, sent out deliveries through companies like Deliveroo, Food Panda, Oddle, and Lalamove, but the problem was that nobody had enough drivers. The demand became too high because, as people staying at home got cabin fever, they craved our food and wanted to escape the day-to day dullness of eating supermarket food. Suddenly, there were mothers whose home space was invaded upon by their husbands and children. Everyone was at home—online work, online school, online university; there was a lot of pressure on the mothers, and they were looking for solutions.

The home delivery strategy worked, and, during April, sales were double that of in March. For us, the sudden shift to takeaway was made possible because, twelve months earlier, Stephanie had insisted that we start looking at packaging for takeaway. We had a delivery component before the pandemic, but it was a very minor part of what we did. Stephanie thought it would be a great idea to repackage our retail items and invest in really high-quality packaging. A little bit like TWG has because they do it beautifully. Each bag of theirs looks like a Gucci bag. What do they sell? Tea. You can buy it in the supermarket for twenty cents, but they put it into their signature bags, and that is branding. I was resistant to the whole thing because it was a $60,000 investment. This was a large investment for F&B for just one category, but Steph's idea was that it is net advertising, so she did not see it as an expense but an investment in our brand. If you ask Stephanie what Wild Honey is, she will answer that it is a communications company rather than a restaurant. So, to her, communicating our brand is essential. People will see the beautiful Wild Honey bag on Orchard Road and voila—it will put the idea in their head, plant a seed, leading hopefully to an order for some takeaway from Wild Honey.

Personally, I hate food delivery, and I would much rather dine in. Our restaurants are all about the experience of dining-in and the ambience, so the challenge was how we will be able to package that experience so it could be taken home. That was something completely new that needed to be created. Stephanie put an enormous amount of research into this. We interviewed the team, and we found out that their number one complaint from customers was spillage. All kinds of experiments on spillage had to be done. Stephanie shadowed the drivers, travelling with them, and saw what it was like to have the food in the backpack. She researched the best kind of materials to keep the heat inside the box so that the food could travel as far as possible for island-wide delivery. Everything was customized and made in China and then shipped to Singapore to save costs. Obviously, almost all of it was recycled as this was very important to us. We already put a lot of effort into the packaging for our inhouse products like jams, honeys, and granola, and now we were expanding to box up our cured lemon, the salsa, the different chili dips, and cakes. We created cake boxes for individual cakes and whole cakes. And what about coffee bags? Each item needed individual packaging, and this had to be developed with care. Then how do you plate into a box? The plating has to remain attractive and needed to resonate with a Wild Honey look rather than something having just been dumped into a box.

There are some very good restaurants in Singapore, and I will not take any names, that cook beautiful food, Italian and French. You would be amazed at how they pack their food. Their packaging is the same packaging used at hawker stalls. Can you imagine people's surprise when they order this really beautiful food, and it comes in a very ordinary container?

It is a horrible anti-climax. The packaging matters; the branding matters, and I think that is why Wild Honey does so well. We look at every single tiny detail when we pack food, and because of all this research and development, we were ready to go in April 2020 when dine-in was stopped with 10,000 pieces of each item of packaging waiting in the kitchens. So, while our competitors were scrambling to try to juggle delivery, Wild Honey was ready to go. What a huge advantage! Stephanie had that foresight and saw delivery as a growing business; it just grew much quicker and faster than we or anyone else expected.

* * *

Being ready, mobilizing, packing material, and new menus—none of this would have made any difference if we had not had support from the government. It was government support first and foremost that got us through the lockdown and enabled us to continue succeeding as a business. The Singapore government legislated to protect us as tenants, so we got free rent from the landlords. The government stepped in and told landlords they needed to pass down the tax rebates for the base rent to their tenants. The service charge and the utilities we had to swallow, but those were manageable. Our landlords from OUE and South Beach were very supportive and waived rents for April and May. It was disappointing for us that the owners of Scotts Square, Wheelock Properties, refused to waive the rentals, especially given that we had paid over six million dollars in rents since 2011 and attracted tens of thousands of people a month into their mall. We were forced to unite with our fellow tenants and sought legal advice.

The next thing scaring us was salary payments and the levies we paid on our foreign workers. This was not just about Wild Honey surviving; we had loyal staff whose families depended on their income. The government stepped in and helped companies with salaries for Singaporean employees. They paid 70 per cent of the salaries for the first month, 60 per cent in the second, and 50 per cent in the third. They refunded us the entire foreign worker levies for April and May. Labour costs are one of Wild Honey's biggest expenditures, so this was a huge help to us. We were also totally refunded all the taxes paid in 2019. This amounted to a return of all the money that we had been paying in taxes for the last ten years. This was a lot of money, and it all came back to us. Thanks to the government, we were able to retain all of our employees and reopen right after the 'circuit breaker' ended. It is very complicated in Singapore because so much support staff comes from Malaysia. So, if we had not been able to hold onto our staff, we would not have been able to reopen. That is what happened with a lot of restaurants because they had to let go of a lot of the staff, so they were unable to reopen.

We could also continue functioning because of all the heroes. In the restaurant world, that meant our suppliers. Without them, how would we have had any food to deliver? Our suppliers saved the day. They supplied the milk and the eggs, and bakers continued to bake the bread, and without them, Wild Honey would have just served air and good wishes. Singapore was able to maintain the logistics of supplying imported foods to the local supermarkets, in your grocers and in your bakers. I do not think people quite understand how much effort it took to achieve that. Incredibly, the entire time, we never ran out of anything, not a single ingredient. I am grateful to Ernst Huber from Hubers in Dempsey, our bakers from Bread Yard, and Common Man Coffee Roasters, who roast their coffee locally here in Singapore. These are the very personal relationships I have built up over the years and proved invaluable. The only people I saw during the lockdown were the Deliveroo and the

Grab people who just tirelessly kept going. The biggest heroes were the medical workers. We would see them at Wild Honey everyday as they came to pick up their food, before or after their shift, and the fatigue and increasing stress on their faces grew daily. Then, of course, there were the security people who worked in the hotel sector, who had to continue regardless and suddenly found their jobs expanded into temperature checkers, screening each visitor, and ensuring no one broke the new restrictions on movement.

My whole world felt upside down, and what was really meaningful for me was that the government, in evaluating each industry, declared restaurants a necessity. We were important, and so Wild Honey needed to stay open. This gave me a tremendous fire and motivation to wake up every morning and go to work. Steph would look at me and ask, 'Where are you going? It's so early. Why rush to the restaurant when it's closed?' I would correct her, 'No it's not closed. We're open. We are open for online. We are open for takeaway.' It was important for me to always have that mindset that we never closed, and I was busy planning for the end of the 'circuit breaker' and the return to in-house dining. We had no idea how that would look yet. Certainly, behaviour around retail and restaurants was going to change after two months of social distancing. Whatever the new paradigm would be, I wanted to be ready.

* * *

After the lockdown was over, things did change dramatically. When we reopened, so many processes had to be updated and changed not just due to new government regulations but due to our customers who were cautiously trying to navigate living with Covid-19. Our innovation came to the rescue again. We were working with a company called Waitrr, which specialized in

QR codes. So, you could come to the restaurant, order through the QR code, and then do takeaway without having to touch the menu or hand over a credit card. Totally contactless. We had introduced this as a pilot before the pandemic because we had our never-ending staffing issues, and this was an efficient and cheap solution.

I thought that it was very promising. Like my initial order-at-the-counter procedure, the reaction to it was lukewarm. Actually, the reaction was cold. However, post-pandemic, most restaurants in Singapore have switched their procedures to scanning QR codes. Enter, scan the QR code for contact tracing, sit down, scan the QR code for the menu and a separate one for drinks. So, before the pandemic we went from a minimal number of transactions per day to all of the transactions at Wild Honey going through this app. I love this technology. It takes away all the tedious tasks the guests have of ordering, paying, and splitting the bill with their friends. It frees us up to do the really fun part, which is to converse with the guests. The hospitality aspect is so important because if we are just really limited to being order-takers, then it makes us like all the other restaurants in Singapore; there is nothing unique about it anymore. Remember my father, Gabriel, at Café Carmel charming the guests? With this technology, we can have efficiency even with high volumes, along with the chance to interact with our guests and make them feel at home.

People are social animals and crave company. So, after the lockdown, they came happily spending their money. Restaurants have become busier than ever, but once again, we needed to be even more creative. There was less supply; seating was initially decreased by 30 per cent, and we were only allowed to seat up to five people at one table. In between, it was limited to two to a table and then back to five again. Whereas earlier we could arrange our tables to seat six, seven, or even twelve, now we need to rearrange the restaurant like a jigsaw puzzle.

At the same time, safety had taken on a new meaning. We had to make sure that we did not have crowding, so that everyone would feel safe, both our guests and our staff. Anxiety levels had gone up. It is easy to serve people when they are in a good mood, but what is really challenging is dealing with anxious and demanding guests. That is when we need to take extra care and pay more attention. That does not cost us anything. In the industry, we call it 'touching the table'. Take the temperature of the table, as we call it. This means making sure that everything is all right on the table, and many a times the problem has nothing to do with the restaurant. The customers may walk in with a situation, and if you do not know how to spot that, you walk onto that landmine, and it can blow up in your face. Covid-19 has created more landmines. In restaurants, on the roads, and in life, people are more stressed and unsure than ever before.

In 2020, restaurants fell like flies and many just did not reopen after the lockdown. The pandemic did not discriminate. Chinese restaurants like Imperial Treasure in Ngee Ann City closed after sixteen years of business, the Japanese cuisine served at Kuishin Bo stopped serving after nineteen years in business, and the cake centric Bakerz Inn shut down island-wide operations after twenty-two years. At Wild Honey, we are just very good at staying ahead of the curve and innovating. I think that the future of F&B is not going to be restaurants per se. Anyone who has a great recipe for a pandan cake or fried chicken will be able to market it and sell that to the consumer. Restaurants will still exist, but the market will be very different. The operators that can innovate and find new platforms and those who seize the new opportunities are going to be the ones leading the way. Covid-19 taught me to expect the unexpected and that you must be a problem solver.

Living and working during the pandemic taught us that we needed to focus our business more on delivery, and in 2021, we were approached by Deliveroo to operate a cloud kitchen on the west coast of Singapore. We had wanted to do this with our South Beach outlet but had been (happily) pressured into opening a fully operational restaurant. So, here was our chance again. We jumped at the opportunity; the investment was minimal because Deliveroo had already secured the real estate and equipment. It was a flexible deal with only a three month commitment, and it was strategically located in an industrial area filled with offices, TV media companies, and film studios. Editions by Deliveroo was a cluster of ten small kitchens combined together in one central location. The location could reach neighbourhoods like Bukit Timah, Holland, Buona Vista, Dover, and Commonwealth. These were fantastic as potential markets for us. All we needed to do was cook delicious food, and Deliveroo would handle the rest!

We opened on 1 April 2021. The onboarding process was very professional, and we were impressed. But alas! This venture was short-lived, and due to severe staffing issues, we were forced to close it just two months later. There were some silver linings though. For instance, we decided to experiment with Israeli street food, and we found a talented Israeli chef working in high tech in Singapore and partnered with him. We already had the experience of working with Chef Yossi and so this felt familiar and fun working on this new menu. We were proud to create a selection of delicious hummus bowls made with tahini oil imported from Israel. This menu will live on, even though our cloud kitchen did not succeed.

* * *

Hospitality has been my life. I believe those early days playing at Café Carmel, the profound influence of my father's creativity, and the impeccable training at Brenner's Park-Hotel were all important precursors to opening Wild Honey in Singapore. Like all good relationships, the business has also hurt and betrayed me at times. After surviving the lockdown, the pressure did not relent. All the coaching and financial support we gave our culinary staff became meaningless when on New Year's Day 2021, a party of seven customers was running late, and the kitchen revolted and threatened to walk out, demanding 13th month bonuses and overtime to keep working. Come 2022 and everything opened up, but part-time staff vanished into thin air—a global problem, not just a Singapore problem. Where did they go, you might ask. Great question. I wish I knew. We had anticipated life returning to normal, and yes, people are flocking back to restaurants but surviving, for smaller businesses like ours, was much, much harder. Unbelievably, post-covid, landlords actively began increasing service charges and rentals in the middle of lease terms, even before retail had the chance to recover. Add to that the fact that smaller restaurants like Wild Honey were paying 30 per cent to delivery platforms and subsidizing fast-food chains who only paid a 5 per cent fee. Being small is not easy.

When the famous restaurateur Danny Meyer was asked in an interview 'How much of your success is based on sheer talent and how much is luck?' he replied, '80 per cent luck and 20 per cent . . . you know, good, good work ethics.' I think that is really true. I have been very lucky to have had the experiences I had, to be in Singapore, and open with the right concept at the right time. I have been lucky to have had so many generous people advise me along the way and, most importantly, to have Stephanie believe in and join me in making Wild Honey a success. I started out by saying that

I hope would-be restaurateurs might learn something from my experiences; instead, the process of writing this book has proved invaluable to me in revealing my next steps in life. I have learned how much I was shaped by my childhood struggles, how passionate I am about the industry, and how I have to keep aiming higher to survive.

We are forever grateful to the Singapore government for their active financial support during the pandemic, and I know restaurants will continue to innovate and adapt, meeting future challenges. However, the climate has changed, and given the difficulties, I foresee dining out becoming increasingly out-of-reach for ordinary people, with food becoming the ultimate luxury. Had we taken the brand as far as it could go? Was this the time for the next step for us? Maybe we could take the brand to Los Angeles where Alex has gone to university, and he would take over the business. Maybe? Wild Honey has the recipe for success, our track record speaks to that, but did we now need a partner to help us—a new venture perhaps or branching out? And as these very thoughts fluttered around in my mind, we were approached by property tycoon Raj Kumar of RB Capital to join forces in a hotel joint-venture project.

Of course, the journey ahead remains uncertain, but as long as Stephanie and I use our gut instincts and continue to be risk-takers, I believe the future, whatever it may bring, will remain bright.

Acknowledgements

Stephanie Hancock for naming the title of this book and her creative input.

My writer, Sumati Sachdev for her constant support and endless rewrites on this book.

My publisher Nora Nazerene Abu Bakar for believing in my story.

My editor Amberdawn Manaois for her professional advice.

My life coach Irena Constantin for encouragement on this book.

Orchard Road Business Association's Steven Goh

Embassy of Israel, Singapore

Jewish Welfare Board, Singapore

Design: Book cover by Alice Good (Goods Lift)

I would like to express my gratitude to our suppliers and partners at:

Olive Grove Kitchens, Dennis, John, Chef Khima
Culina, Dennis Lim and team
Common Man Coffee Roasters, Jake, Mathew, Carmin,
Quen Mei Construction, Steven Lew and team
OUE, Patrina Tan, Jessica Lim

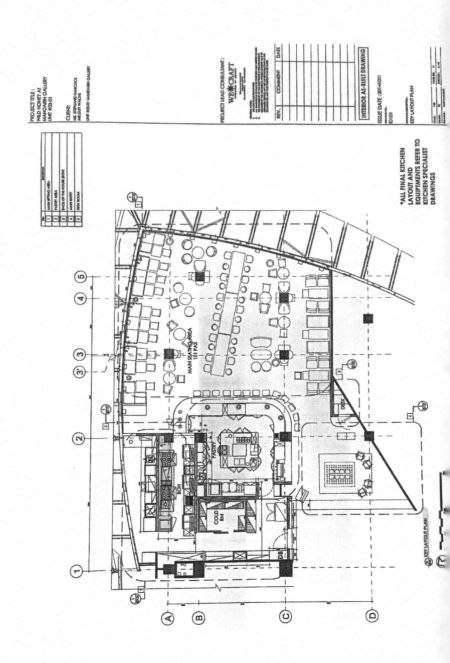

PROJECT TITLE:
WILD HONEY AT
MANDARIN GALLERY
UNIT #03-01

CLIENT:
MS. STEPHANIE HANCOCK
MR. GUY WACHS
UNIT #03-01 MANDARIN GALLERY

PROJECT LEAD CONSULTANT:
WERKCRAFT

INTERIOR AS-BUILT DRAWING
ISSUE DATE : 20141031
ID101
KEY LAYOUT PLAN

*ALL FINAL KITCHEN
LAYOUT AND
EQUIPMENTS REFER TO
KITCHEN SPECIALIST
DRAWINGS

REV.	COMMENT	DATE

MAIN SEATING AREA
101 PAX

BOH

COLD
RM

PASTRY

DB

KEY LAYOUT PLAN